WORSHIP

IN SPIRIT AND TRUTH

WORSHIP

IN SPIRIT AND TRUTH

Stephen Kaung

Christian Fellowship Publishers, Inc.

New York

Large Print ISBN: 978-1-68062-129-7
Paperback ISBN: 978-1-68062-113-6
eBook ISBN: 978-1-68062-114-3

Available from the Publishers at:

11515 Allecingie Parkway
Richmond, Virginia 23235
www.c-f-p.com

Printed in the United States of America

Preface

Being created by God, it is but right and natural for us to worship God. If we worship God, we will find our fulfillment. But unfortunately, there is an enemy, and this enemy is trying to steal that worship which is God's due. He is trying to lead us away from worshiping God into worshiping him. That is the reason worship is the center of a tremendous conflict that is going on in this world today.

In these seven messages on worship, we see the heart of worship as well as the regular practice. We look into the question: What is worship? And then we discover how worship is experienced in the breaking of bread and prayer.

The hour is coming and now is, when the true worshippers shall worship the Father in spirit and truth; for also the Father seeks such as his worshippers (John 4:23).

Our Heavenly Father is seeking true worshipers. God alone is to be worshiped. It is true—it will be costly. We will be tempted and assaulted. But thank God, our Lord Jesus has already overcome. And as His overcoming life is in us, so we too will overcome and worship God.

Contents

Note

In 1980 seven messages on worship were delivered by the author before a group of Christians gathered together in Richmond, VA. The texts of these messages were recorded and later transcribed and lightly edited for publication.

Unless otherwise indicated, Scripture quotations are from the *New Translation* by J. N. Darby.

1—Worship in Spirit and Truth

John 4:19-30—The woman says to him, Sir, I see that thou art a prophet. Our fathers worshiped in this mountain, and ye say that in Jerusalem is the place where one must worship. Jesus says to her, Woman, believe me, the hour is coming when ye shall neither in this mountain nor in Jerusalem worship the Father. Ye worship ye know not what; we worship what we know, for salvation is of the Jews. But the hour is coming and now is, when the true worshipers shall worship the Father in spirit and truth; for also the Father seeks such as his worshipers. God is a spirit; and they who worship him must worship him in spirit and truth. The woman says to him, I know that Messias is coming, who is called Christ; when he comes he will tell us all things. Jesus says to her, I who speak to thee am he. And upon this came his disciples, and wondered that he spoke with a woman; yet no one said, What seekest thou? or, Why speakest thou with her? The woman then left her waterpot and went away into the city, and says to the men, Come, see a man who told me all things I had ever done: is not he the Christ? They went out of the city and came to him.

Our Lord Jesus was leaving Judea for Galilee, and the Bible says that He must pass through Samaria. While He was in Samaria, He sat by the well of Jacob, and at noontime, a woman came to draw water. The Lord began to talk with her, humbling himself by asking for water. The woman was so prejudiced against the Jews that she did not want to give water to the Lord, so He offered her living water. During the conversation, the Lord brought out the sins that she had committed and was still living in, and as she was being awakened spiritually, she said, "Sir, You must be a prophet. Tell me about worship. We worship in Mt. Gerizim, and the Jews worship in the temple in Jerusalem."

When you read the Bible, sometimes you wonder how the Lord could discuss this matter of worship with a woman who lived in sin and who had just been awakened spiritually. Certainly, He should have talked to Nicodemus about this. He should have told this woman about the new birth because she was a sinner and talked to Nicodemus about worship because he was a theologian. But our Lord Jesus did not discuss worship with Nicodemus; on the contrary, He discussed worship with a sinner because worship is not an academic subject. It is a spiritual experience. As soon as anyone is awakened spiritually, the first thing that will enter their mind is: How do I worship? Man is created to be a worshiper. God created him with an instinct to worship, and, of course, that instinct should be towards the true God. Worship is built into man. Whenever our conscience is awakened, immediately the question will be: How should I worship? Who should I worship?

Therefore, as soon as this Samaritan woman's conscience was awakened, she immediately went to this matter of worship; but she was confused. Jacob's well was by Mt. Gerizim. Why did they worship there? History tells us that during the time when Nehemiah returned to Jerusalem, he found that the grandson of the high priest, Eliashib, had become son-in-law to Sanballat the Horonite, the Persian satrap of Samaria (see Nehemiah 13). In other words, this grandson of the high priest, in violation of God's law, married a Samaritan and, because of this impurity, Nehemiah chased him out. This grandson went to his father-in-law, Sanballat, who made him the high priest of the temple which he built on Mt. Gerizim because the Samaritans would not have anything to do with the Jews nor the Jews with the Samaritans. Therefore, they built their own temple on Mt. Gerizim and worshiped God there.

We know that the Samaritans believed the Pentateuch, the five books of Moses, which was their Bible. They did not accept the prophets, only the Pentateuch, and they twisted what was written there. God told Moses to command the children of Israel as they entered into the promised land to set up great stones, and plaster them with plaster, and write upon them all the words of this law (see Deuteronomy 27:2b;3a). In their Samaritan Bible, they changed the mount from Mt. Ebal to Mt. Gerizim. They said the law was written on Mt. Gerizim; therefore, that must be the place of worship. Also, after the children of Israel entered the promised land, six of the tribes would stand on Mt. Gerizim and bless the people, and six of the tribes would stand on Mt. Ebal and curse.

So they said Mt. Gerizim is the mountain of blessing. Based on these things, they built the temple on Mt. Gerizim and said it was the place of worship. Since that time, the Samaritans, instead of going to Jerusalem to worship, worshiped on Mt. Gerizim. Of course, we know the temple was destroyed two hundred years later, but the Samaritans continued to worship on Mt. Gerizim.

This Samaritan woman said, "I know I should worship; but where should I worship? It has become so confusing. We say we should worship on Mt. Gerizim, and we have that long tradition before us that has some kind of scriptural foundation (according to their interpretation), but you Jews say you must worship in the temple."

Worship Under the Old Covenant

Why did the Jews say this? In Deuteronomy 12, God commanded Moses that the children of Israel—after they entered into the promised land—should destroy all the idols, all the high places, all the statues and all the groves, the tall trees. The seven tribes of Canaan worshiped many idols on the mountains, in the hills, and under their high trees. God would choose one place out of the whole land to set His name, and the children of Israel must go there to offer sacrifices. They could not do what they did in the wilderness and offer sacrifices wherever they traveled. We know that later on, God chose Jerusalem, but because it was not yet chosen in Deuteronomy, the Samaritans could say Mt. Gerizim was the place. But when you come to the prophets, it is very clear that it is Jerusalem God chose to be the place of worship, and the children of Israel must go there to offer sacrifices and worship God. Three times a year, every male must travel to Jerusalem to offer sacrifices and worship. This was the law.

Why is it that God commanded them in such a way? Why didn't He allow them to worship wherever they wanted? Under the law, the people did not have an inward relationship with God, and if He allowed them to worship wherever they wanted, they would worship whomever they wanted and fall into idolatry and abomination. We find this in the history of Israel—how they began to worship different gods in many places, committed abominations before God, and, finally, had to go into captivity. So under the old covenant, the Samaritans worshiped in Mt. Gerizim according to their tradition, and the Jews worshiped in Jerusalem in the temple according to the word of God.

The Samaritan woman was confused, but is not worship a very confusing problem even to us today? Throughout the world, God's people are worshiping the one God, and yet there are so many forms and kinds of worship. This has confused us. We do not know how to worship God. In the Old Testament times, worship was limited to a place. The Samaritans went to Mt. Gerizim, and the Jews went to the temple in Jerusalem. And because it was limited in place, it must be limited in time since you cannot stay in Mt. Gerizim or the temple all your life. Also, worship that is limited to place and time cannot be perfect.

Furthermore, in the Old Testament time, the knowledge of God was also restricted. They knew God as the Creator and maybe as a deliverer, but they did not know God as Father. In other words, their concept of God was that He is transcendent, far, far above all; therefore, you must worship afar off with fear and trembling, with awe and reverence. There is not that intimacy; there is not that closeness; there is not that relationship of Father and children. This was not known in the Old Testament times. It was not revealed. Therefore, in the Old Testament times, worship was very limited in time, in place, in knowledge, in every way. It was external; it was legal; it was remote. That was the nature of worship under the Old Covenant Law.

Now, as the Lord was conversing with this woman, He said, "Woman, believe me, the hour is coming when ye shall neither in this mountain nor in Jerusalem worship the Father. ... But the hour is coming and now is, when the true worshipers shall worship the Father in spirit and truth" (John 4:21, 23).

As we come to this matter of worship, first of all, we need to see a change of dispensation. The Lord said, "The hour is coming." What hour does He refer to? It is the hour of the change of dispensation. In other words, before the coming of Christ, it was the dispensation of law, and under that, there was a way to worship, but now Christ has come, and the dispensation has changed. It is no longer the law; it has become the dispensation of grace. At the very time when our Lord was talking to the Samaritan woman, the time had changed. He said that the hour has come, and now is. Because of that, the dispensation had changed. Therefore, the very nature of worship and the way to worship also changed.

Worship Under the New Covenant

Under the law, a Jew must worship in Jerusalem in the temple. If he tried to worship somewhere else, it was an abomination in the sight of God. He would be completely rejected by God. Under their tradition, a Samaritan must worship on Mt. Gerizim, and if he did not, he was not a good Samaritan. But the time has changed! Our Lord has come into this world and, with His coming, it is neither Jew nor Samaritan; it is all mankind. It is neither Mt. Gerizim nor the temple in Jerusalem. The very character of worship has undergone a tremendous change. It is no longer the *old*; it is altogether new. Under the New Covenant, worship is based upon a new relationship—the relationship of Father and children. When our Lord Jesus came into this world, he brought to it a new knowledge of God as our Father. Before He came, God was God to mankind. He was their Creator, but now the Lord has revealed the Father to us. Throughout His life, that was what He was doing. He said, "No one has ever seen God, but if one should see Him who is in the bosom of the Father, then he has seen God. If you have seen Me, you have seen the Father" (see John 1:18).

Not only does He reveal the Father to us, but after His resurrection, He told the woman: "Go to my brethren and say to them, I ascend to my Father and your Father, and my God and your God" (John

20:17b). It is through the work of His redemption that He has not only made God known to us as our Father, but He has made God our Father. Today, God is *really* our Father, and we are *really* His children. This is the living relationship that people never knew under the Old Covenant. It is something completely new. Even when the Lord taught us to pray, He said, "Our Father who art in heaven." Your Father seeth it in secret, and He shall reward you. Today, under the New Covenant in Christ, we find that our relationship with God is more than Him being God to us. Of course, He is still God; He is our Maker, our Creator; but He is more than that—He is also our Father. There is an intimate relationship established. Under the Old Covenant, people worshiped God as God, but under the New Covenant, we worship God as our Father. It is entirely different. When you worship God as One who is transcendent, you have to worship afar off. You dare not draw too close. You cannot. It has to be remote, distant. But if you worship your Father, you draw near to Him. You worship Him in love, not in fear. Our worship is based on a new relationship—Father and children.

Also, under the Old Covenant, worship was limited in place. You could not worship anywhere you wanted. You had to go to the appointed place, which was Jerusalem, and not only that, you had to go to the temple. If you were a Samaritan, you would have to go to Mt. Gerizim to be a good Samaritan. However, under the New Covenant, it is no longer so. It is neither the mountain nor the temple because worship has become a spiritual thing; we worship in spirit and truth. And if it is in spirit and in reality, then there is no limit to place and no restriction of time. It has to be worship in spirit and truth.

How does worship happen in Christianity today? Do we understand the nature of worship in Christ? How often we find in Christianity that people are worshiping God in the Old Testament way because people think God is a God who is billions and billions of miles away. They think He is transcendent, that He is not imminent, and therefore in order to worship Him, they have to have a place. There is a place called *the place of worship*. If they want to worship God, they go to that place of worship. If there is a place of worship, then there is a *time of worship.* When? On Sunday, of course! What time do they worship? There is an hour called *the hour of worship.* They have a worship service, and that is the time when people come and worship. In other words, after worship, they can do anything they like.

True Worshipers

How do people worship? They worship with rituals and ceremonies. They have to have a building which is built in a special way. They must have a special atmosphere, created with darkness, with dimness, with light, with candles, with incense, with music, with all kinds of things trying to draw out from people a kind of worship. They use all kinds of postures to express that worship. They have to have a program to stir up worship.

Are we worshiping God in the Old Testament way, or are we worshiping God in the New Testament way? The hour has come, and now is when the Father is seeking true worshipers—those who will worship Him in spirit and in truth. The word *true* not only means "it is true" but "it is complete," or probably the nearest translation will be "ideal." The Father is seeking *ideal* worshipers, those who worship the Father in spirit and truth.

God's people are supposed to worship God, yet we worship Him in a way that is like the Old Testament times. How sad this is. If we are doing that in such a way, do you think that we are *ideal* worshipers? Do you think this is the worship that our Father is seeking? Do you think that our Father will be pleased to see that His children are worshiping far, far away as strangers with fear and trembling? Do you think the Father will accept such worship? Do you think God is worshiped today? If we go back to the word of God, how much is God our Father really being worshiped by His people today? The Father is seeking true worshipers—those who worship Him in spirit and truth.

God is Spirit

Augustine said that God is a Spirit. If God is physical, having a body, then it is right to worship God on a mountain. If God has a body, then it is right to worship God in a temple because the mountain is a corporeal thing, and so is the temple. But God is not a body; God is a Spirit; therefore, those who worship Him must worship Him in spirit. Now, of course, when the Bible says God is a Spirit, it does not refer to the personality of God. It refers to the essence of God. God, in essence, is Spirit, and those who worship Him must worship in spirit. This was impossible under the Old Covenant. This was impossible in the old days. This was impossible for people before Christ came because they were all dead in sins and transgressions.

What does it mean to be dead in sins and trans-gressions? When Paul wrote the letter to the, Ephesians saying we were dead in sins and transgressions (see 2:1), he was talking to the

Ephesians, and they were very much alive at that time. You cannot talk to a dead man because he cannot hear. So when Paul said we were dead in sins and transgressions, he was referring to the Ephesians who were living. He means that because we have sinned, our spirit is dead to God.

In the garden of Eden, God told Adam that in the day he ate the forbidden fruit, he would surely die (see Genesis 2:17b). Adam and Eve ate, and they lived in their physical bodies for hundreds of years. But they were *dead* on the very day they ate the forbidden fruit. They were dead in sins and transgressions since their spirit was dead in them.

God had created man with a spirit, and in man's spirit, there is an instinct called communion, called worship. God created man as a worshiper and gave him the ability to worship, and because God is a spirit and man was created with a spirit, it is with that spirit that man can commune with God and worship Him. But the moment man sinned, the spirit was dead to

God. In other words, the contact was cut off. Yet, deep down within man, there was still that sense of worship. Even though the spirit was dead to God, it was still there as an organ. It had lost its contact with God; it could not worship God; it was damaged. However, there was still that trace, that instinct of worship; so, instead of worshiping God, they began to worship the devil and idols of all kinds. Since the spirit was dead to God, they could not worship Him spiritually, so they tried to worship Him in physical ways with their bodies. They also tried to worship God with their souls. But since they were dead spiritually, they could not contact God and worship Him in spirit. They could only worship God afar off, never in closeness. This was the Old Testament times.

Worship in Spirit

Thank God, our Lord Jesus has come and has finished the work of redemption on Calvary's cross! With that finished work, our dead spirit is made alive again to

God. This is new birth. He that is born of the Spirit is spirit (see John 3:6). The first thing that happens to us after we believe in the Lord Jesus and our sins are forgiven is that the spirit, which was formerly dead in sins and transgressions, is quickened by the Holy Spirit into a new spirit and, immediately we cry out, "Abba Father." Immediately our spirit is in touch with God the Spirit, and worship begins.

Today, we are able to worship God as our Father because our spirit is renewed and awakened. Therefore, under the New Covenant, we worship our Father in spirit. It is now possible. In other words, we do not worship God in the flesh anymore. In the old days, people worshiped God in the flesh; that is, they worshiped with their body and soul without the spirit. That is the fallen man. If we worship God with our body, we will have to have all these rituals to help us. People have to prostrate themselves; they have to have different postures; they have to create a kind of sense or imagination; they have to "cook up" a kind of concept in order to worship God. People use all these aids to worship God in the flesh but not in the spirit.

Our Lord Jesus said, "This people honor me with the lips, but their heart is far away from me; but in vain do they worship me" (Matthew 15:8-9a). Today, worship is no longer in the flesh; it is worship in the spirit. Our spirit, being renewed and awakened unto God, is now in contact with God and, out of our spirit, we worship God the Spirit. It is beyond the physical, beyond the psychological, beyond emotion, beyond intelligence, beyond the will.

Colossians mentions "*will* worship" (see 2:23 KJV). People can worship God by *will* worship. In other words, we *will* to worship God, and we *will* that this is the way God should be worshiped. *Will* worship is not true worship.

This does not mean that if we worship in the spirit, our soul and body are not involved. Of course they are! Our spirit needs to come out through our soul and body, but it has to originate from the spirit. Naturally, we have to use our lips (part of the body). Otherwise, how can we offer God the sacrifice of praise? We have to praise God with our mouth, with our lips. Some people say they will worship God in the spirit; therefore, they will not open their mouths; they will not utter a word. They are wrong. It is true, you have to worship from your spirit, but it has to be uttered through your lips, your body. That is the sacrifice of praise unto God. The body is also involved, though it originates from the spirit.

We cannot say that since we worship God in spirit, emotion is not involved. This is not so at all. But does it originate from the soulical emotion or does it originate from the spirit? If it comes from the spirit, it ought to touch your emotion, and it should be expressed through your emotion.

The same thing is true with your mind, your thought. If you are trying to create some noble or lofty thoughts, stirring up your imagination, having a mental image of Christ and His cross, and things like that to worship God, then something is wrong. It is just like having to use a crucifix to stir up your sympathy for Christ. That is wrong. But it is not wrong if in your spirit there is contact with God and you begin to worship, and it comes out in your thoughts. This is proper and right.

The same thing is true with the will. If it originates with your will, it is wrong, but if it originates from your spirit and your will wills the will of God, then you are willing to cooperate; and that is right. Sometimes, you come to worship, and you will (or choose) to not open your mouth. You do not cooperate. You have to will the will of God. You do have to will (choose) to worship God, but the worship itself must come forth from the spirit. Remember, we worship God in spirit.

Heart Worship

If you do not quite understand the word *spirit,* then use the word that you do understand—*heart*. The Lord Jesus said the Pharisees worshiped God with their lips, but their heart was not involved; therefore, they worshiped God in vain. When we worship God, our heart must be in it. Whether we sing or whether we pray, our heart must be there. If our heart is not involved, it is lip service. It is not "worship in spirit." That is the reason we need to prepare our hearts before we come together. Be sure that your heart is right with God. Be sure that your heart is in tune with Him. Be sure that your heart is touched by His love, that it is not a hardened heart through the deceitfulness of sin throughout the week, but it is a heart of flesh, a tender heart towards God.

What is worship in spirit? It is in contrast with worship in letter. In the Old Testament times, in Judaism, they worshiped in letter—"This is the way to do things." But today, we are to worship God in spirit.

It is no longer a matter of formality. If we worship God in letter, then it is a formality. Everything is programmed, but it is dead. We worship God in spirit, not in letter.

Worship in spirit and Spirit

"We are the true circumcision who worship God in Spirit and have no confidence in the flesh" (Philippians 3:3). There are two different translations to this verse. The first one is that we worship God in spirit; that is, we exercise our spirit to worship God and not just our body or our mind. Another translation is that we worship God by the Spirit of God. In the New Testament, sometimes it is very difficult to distinguish between the human spirit and the Holy Spirit. The human spirit and the Holy Spirit are so much together that sometimes you cannot distinguish them. But still, we must worship God in spirit.

In John 4, the word *spirit* is written with a small letter. That is the interpretation of the translator. When the Bible was written, it was either in all small or all capital letters; so, whether it is a capital or a small letter will depend on the interpretation. Here the interpreters felt it was the human spirit. Therefore it says, "We worship God in spirit" (small letter). And that is true.

In Philippians 3, you will find a difficulty. Some translators felt it should be the Spirit of God and others thought that it should be the human spirit. Therefore, you have two different translations. They are both right. Worshiping God in spirit does mean you worship God by the Spirit of God. There is a tremendous difference here. If we say we worship God in spirit and forget the Holy Spirit, we get into big difficulties, great confusion. In the first place, we do not know our spirit. Do you know your spirit? Remember the story of the two sons of Zebedee. As the Lord was going through the Samaritan villages, because he was headed towards Jerusalem, the Samaritans would not receive our Lord. The two sons of Zebedee came to the Lord and said, "They do not receive You. Do You want us to ask God to send fire from Heaven to burn them up?" The Lord Jesus said, "You do not know what kind of spirit you have" (see Luke 9:51-55).

We say we worship in spirit, which means that whenever our human spirit wants to do something, we do it. But do we know our spirit? We do not know our spirit because from our spirit can come forth that which is of God or that which is from ourselves. We do not know how to control our spirit. Now some people say that we should be controlled by our spirit, but actually, we should be controlled by the Holy Spirit, not by our own spirit. In Proverbs 16:32, it says, "He that rules over his spirit is better than he that overcomes a city." In other words, it is not easy to rule over your spirit. It is a great thing if you can control your spirit. "The spirits of the prophets are subject to the prophets" (I Corinthians 14:32). Therefore, we worship in spirit, but it is in cooperation with the Spirit of God. It is the Spirit of God that touches our spirit, and that is where it begins. It does not originate with our spirit; it originates with the Spirit of God. Because the Spirit of God dwells in our spirit, He makes His mind known to our spirit. He makes His impression upon our spirit, and as our spirit receives the impression from God the Spirit, then we are moved by the Spirit of God. This is the way we worship. In the New Testament time, we worship in spirit. It is not an external matter; it is an inward one. It is not a form; it is a spiritual thing.

Worship in Truth

The Bible says God is seeking for worshipers, true worshipers who worship Him in spirit and truth. When we quote this verse, we often say, "… who worship God in spirit and *in* truth," but the second *in* is not there. There is a difference here. It is one complex phrase, not two coordinated phrases. In other words, we tend to divide the spirit and the truth. It is true, there is a distinction, but you cannot divide them. You cannot separate them. If you do, you have problems. It has to be spirit and truth. We often think of spirit as subjective, truth as objective, and in a sense, that is true.

What is worship? Someone said that worship is based on two things. One is a feeling, the other is a concept. Worship is an inward feeling and that is in spirit. But worship is also a concept; there is an object towards which your feeling is directed. Therefore, on one hand, there is feeling within you and on the other hand, there is an object before you. That feeling is in spirit; that concept is in truth. In other words, when we worship, we must know whom we are worshiping. Of the Samaritans it is said, "Ye worship ye know not what" (John 4:22). It is false worship. We must know whom we worship, and that is why it says we must worship in truth.

What is truth? There are two things we can mention about truth. Truth is the word of God. In John 17 it says, "Sanctify them by the truth: thy word is truth." When we worship God, we have to worship according to truth. The Samaritans worshiped according to tradition, the teaching of men, their fathers. It was false. They were not worshiping in truth. The Jews worshiped according to the law which is truth, and yet, they did not worship in spirit. But we, who have been redeemed of the Lord, have the spirit as well as the truth. So today, if we want to worship our Father, we have to worship according to truth, that is, according to the word of God. You are not free to worship in whatever way you want or according to your own ideas. We must worship God according to His word.

In John 14, the Lord said, "I am the truth" (verse 6). In other words, it is not just a written word. Now, of course, that is the basis of our worship. How do we know Him whom we worship? It is through the word of God. If there is not the word, we do not know whom we are worshiping. All our knowledge of God is through the word; therefore, it has to be based on the word. But truth is something more. Truth is a Person; it is our Lord himself; He is the truth. This written word through revelation becomes the living Word to us. If it is just the word and there is no revelation, it is letter and the letter kills. But the written word with the revelation from above becomes the living Word. It is Christ; He is the truth. So, as we worship the Father, we worship Him in the reality of Christ. Or to put it in another way, as we worship the Father, we are giving back to Him that revelation of Christ which He has given to us. This is the spiritual sacrifice that the Bible talks about. We are not worshiping Him with our self, with our works. If we do, it is like Cain offering the produce of the fields. We are worshiping God with the Christ that has been made real to us through the revelation of the Holy Spirit. That is worship.

Under the New Covenant, through the finished work of Christ, our worship today is entirely different from the worship of the past. We worship God not only as God transcendent, but also as God imminent; not only as Creator, but also as our Father. God is looking for His sons to worship Him, and this is our basis of worship. As we worship, we worship in spirit and truth; not only in *spirit* but *in spirit and truth*; not only in *truth* but *in spirit and truth*.

Often, when we worship, we have many feelings, but there is very much lacking in substance, in concepts. By concepts, I do not mean mental concepts but revealed knowledge, experiential knowledge of God. Because we do not have much life with Christ, even though we may have much feeling, it is very empty. God is not worshiped as He should be. On the other hand, we may have a great knowledge of God, but we may not have any feeling towards Him. If that is the case, it is dead; it is not living, and our Father is not worshiped. Oh, how we need to see that as we come to worship, it is in spirit and truth and, because of that, there is that going out of our heart in love and adoration. Also, there is that substance that we can bring to the Father, that knowledge of Christ that He has revealed to us through the week or through the days, and if that is the case, the Father is worshiped.

The Lord said, "But the hour is coming and now is, when the true worshipers shall worship the Father in spirit and truth" (John 4:23). The time has changed, therefore we shall not worship in the old way—in Jerusalem or Mt. Gerizim. We worship in spirit and truth. Then the Lord said, "For also the Father seeks such as his worshipers ... and they who worship him must worship him in spirit and truth" (John 4:23a,24b). Not only has the time changed but also the nature of worship has changed; therefore, any worship that is not in spirit and truth is not true worship. May we be true worshipers.

After the Samaritan woman heard from the Lord about worship, she left her waterpot which she had brought and went to the city and said, "Come, see a man who told me all things I had ever done." Through her witness, many in the city came to the Lord. The Samaritan woman had become a worshiper because worship was no more a matter of place or time. Worship is a life; worship is service; worship is testimony. So the Lord changed that Samaritan woman from a sinner into a worshiper. Now if the Lord can do it with a Samaritan woman, certainly He can do it with all of us.

2—What is Worship?

Genesis 22:5—And Abraham said to his young men, Abide ye here with the ass; and I and the lad will go yonder and worship, and come again to you.

Revelation 5:6-14—And I saw in the midst of the throne and of the four living creatures, and in the midst of the elders, a Lamb standing, as slain, having seven horns and seven eyes, which are the seven Spirits of God which are sent into all the earth: and it came and took it out of the right hand of him that sat upon the throne. And when it took the book, the four living creatures and the twenty-four elders fell before the Lamb, having each a harp and golden bowls full of incenses, which are the prayers of the saints. And they sing a new song, saying, Thou art worthy to take the book, and to open its seals; because thou hast been slain, and hast redeemed to God, by thy blood, out of every tribe, and tongue, and people, and nation, and made them to our God kings and priests; and they shall reign over the earth.

And I saw, and I heard the voice of many angels around the throne and the living creatures and the elders; and their number was ten thousands of ten thousands and thousands of thousands; saying with a loud voice, Worthy is the Lamb that has been slain, to receive power, and riches, and wisdom, and strength, and honour, and glory, and blessing. And every creature which is in the heaven and upon the earth and under the earth, and those that are upon the sea, and all things in them, heard I saying, To him that sits upon the throne, and to the Lamb, blessing, and honour, and glory, and might, to the ages of ages. And the four living creatures said, Amen; and the elders fell down and did worship.

Worship is not a theological matter; worship is a spiritual experience. Everyone whose conscience has been awakened by the Spirit of God will turn to this matter of worship, and everyone who is redeemed by the precious blood of the Lamb is qualified to be a worshiper—a true worshiper of the Father.

It is very strange that in the Bible, in the word of God, you rarely have any definition of worship. The Bible does not define things as we want them to be. The truth that is in the Bible is so inclusive that it is impossible to define. When you try to define a thing, in a sense, you confine it. Worship is found every-where in the Bible, yet it is never defined. And proba-bly, this is one reason why we have such a vague idea of what worship is. Modern man likes to see things defined in concrete terms, then we can understand them and we can grasp them. But spiritual things are beyond human comprehension. So the best way to understand worship is not in trying to define it, but in seeing how worship is illustrated in the Bible. In other words, you do not have the definition of worship in the Bible but you have plenty of examples, and I think we learn by example more than by definition. So if the Lord enables us, we will go through the whole Bible in a very rapid way to find some of these examples.

What is worship? How do we worship? On what occasion do we worship? At what time do we worship? What kind of worship really touches God's heart?

Examples of Worship in the Old Testament

Abraham

We often say the first mention of a word in the Bible gives somewhat of a clue. The word worship in the Old Testament is the Hebrew word *shachah*, and the first mention of it is in Genesis 22:5. Abraham told the young men: "Stay here and I and the lad will go yonder and worship and then return." The word *worship* in Hebrew means "bow self down; to bow one's self low and down." Of course, it does not mean that before Abraham worshiped God that God was not worshiped at all. No doubt, when Abel offered the lamb on the altar, he worshiped God. Noah, also, after he came out of the ark, built an altar and the sweet-smelling savor went up to God. But the first mention of the word worship is found in Genesis 22:5 because this incident reveals to us the very essence of worship.

Abraham had a long life with God and, through his long experience, he knew God in a very deep way. God revealed himself to Abraham in a way that He had never done with anyone before him. But then God tested Abraham. He said, "Abraham, offer your son Isaac to me, your only son" (see Genesis 22:2). Without hesitation, Abraham rose up early in the morning, took his son Isaac and traveled three days' journey to Mt. Moriah. God gave him enough time to think things over, but his heart was fixed upon God. He never looked back. When he arrived at the foot of the mountain, he told the young men to stay behind. That was very wise because he was going to do something that, humanly speaking, was abhorrent. He said, "I and the lad will go yonder and worship." How did Abraham worship God? He worshiped God by offering his only begotten son, Isaac. He did not hold back anything from God. He considered God as worthy of his very best. God was worthy not only of his sheep and his cattle, but He was worthy even of his only begotten son, in whom was all his hope. He considered God as more worthy than his son. Of course, we know the story. He bound his son, laid him on the altar, and when he took up the knife, he heard a voice say, "Abraham, Abraham!" He looked around and saw the ram caught in the thicket, so he offered that ram instead of his son. God was so pleased with him and blessed him. This is worship.

In old English, the word *worship* is spelled "worthship"; and that is very true. Worship comes out of worthship because you consider Him as worthy; therefore, you worship Him. But here, worship is not a matter of a word; it is an act. Often, we think of worship only in terms of a word, such as when we sing, when we pray, or when we praise, we are worshiping God. Of course, when we worship, we do sing, we do pray, and we do praise Him. These are all expressions of worship; but worship is more than just words. Worship must be an act. Abraham worshiped God through an act, and that act proved that God is worthy—more worthy than anything else, and he was willing to give up everything to honor and glorify God. That is worship. And the result of worship is blessing. As Abraham worshiped God with such devotion, God blessed him with such blessings that even all the nations shall be blessed through his seed.

Abraham's Steward

The second mention of worship in the Bible is in Genesis 24. Abraham sent his steward to his native land to get a wife for his son Isaac. The steward traveled to Padan-Aram, and when he arrived there, he prayed as he stood by a well: "O God of Abraham, my master, prosper me and send me to the home of my master's relatives that I might get a wife for my master's son." As he finished his prayer, Rebecca came. He tested her, and when he discovered that she was of his master's family, immediately he worshiped God beside the well. He bowed down and worshiped God (see v. 26) because He had prospered him, He had answered his prayer, He had blessed his master, and He led him to his master's kindred. Then the steward went into their home and told them the story of how God had prospered his way. When the whole thing was settled with Rebecca's relatives, he again worshiped God (see v. 52).

Worship is because God is above all. Worship is because God has provided and prospered. Often, we receive God's grace, and we just take what He has given and walk away. We never return to give thanks to Him. We forget everything. We are ungrateful, and that hurts the heart of God. What is worship? It is when you receive something from God, when He answers your prayer, when He has made provision for you, when He has blessed you and you return to Him to give thanks, telling Him how you appreciate what He has done.

Job

Chronologically speaking, we should mention Job because he lived in the time of the patriarchs. This man Job was perfect, feared God, was upright and God used him to challenge Satan. God said, "Have you seen my servant Job? There is no one more

righteous than he. He fears God, abstains from evil"
(see Job 1:8).

And Satan said, "Is there not a reason why Job fears
You? You have put a hedge around him; You have
blessed him; You have protected him. If You take
away the hedge and let me attack him and take away
all the things You have given to him, then we will
see."

God said, "All right, go ahead, but do not touch his
body." So Satan attacked Job—attack upon attack. He
took away not only his cattle and herds but all his
children. This news came in one day, one after
another, and after Job heard all these calamities, he
rose up, rent his garment, shaved his head, and
bowed down and worshiped God. He said, "God has
given; God has taken; blessed be the name of the
Lord." This is worship.

Worship is not only something you do when God has
blessed you, given you something, or provided for

you, but worship happens especially when everything is taken from you, yet you realize God has the right to take it away. Sometimes, we think it is easier to worship God when He gives, even though often we are not that grateful; but when He begins to take away things from us, can we worship? Will we not rather murmur and sometimes rebel against Him? If we only worship God when He gives or blesses but cannot worship Him when He takes things away or afflicts us, we do not know what worship is. Worship does not depend upon things; worship depends upon God himself. If worship is dependent upon things, and you only worship when God gives you something, then who do you worship? You do not worship God. You worship the things that you have received. But when God takes away your things, and you can still worship, then you see Him; you see God as God, having every right to give and every right to take away. Blessed be the name of the Lord! That is worship.

Towards the end of the book of Job when God revealed himself to him as the Creator, Job said, "I repent in dust and ashes. I realize You are God. You can do anything. No one can say, 'Why do you do it?' You are God." The very acknowledgment of God as God, and the very realization that we are but dust and ashes, is worship. Worship is seeing God as God and seeing ourselves as the dust of the earth.

Jacob

You remember that Jacob worshiped, even though the word worship concerning him was used in the New Testament instead of the Old Testament. In Hebrews 11, we are told that Jacob, before he died, worshiped God leaning on the top of his staff. That staff of his was really something! In Genesis, you read that he said, "For with my staff I passed over this Jordan" (Genesis 32:10b). In other words, when he left home, he had nothing but a staff, and with this staff, he crossed the river. This staff was his very livelihood; it was his cleverness. And with this staff, he maneuvered for twenty years, staying with his uncle Laban. With this staff, he tried to build his own house. He leaned upon it for his very living. It was his cleverness, his strength—symbolic of his life. But God transformed that staff through much dealing with Jacob. God dealt with him again and again and again until it was consummated at the ford of Jabbok, where his thigh was touched and he was crippled. That staff became a symbol of the cross instead of being a sign of his own cleverness and strength. The cross had worked so much in his life that from then on he leaned upon that staff, that cross. He could not live without the cross, and even when he was dying, he leaned on the top of that staff and worshiped God.

Who knows worship? It is not someone who lives in the energy of his own flesh. If you live your life by the strength of your flesh, you worship yourself; you do not know how to worship God. It is only those who have known the cross who can worship God. When the cross works deeply into your life, you begin to realize how weak you are and how strong God is. It is through the working of the cross in your life that you are able to lean upon the top of the staff and worship. When the cross works in our lives, it is painful. It reveals the worst in us. It exposes us completely. But if you allow the cross to perfect its work in you, you will become a true worshiper of God. You begin to realize that it is the cross that gives you Christ. It is the cross that gives you the knowledge of God, and you will lean upon the cross and worship God.

Hannah

Hannah worshiped God. We know how God shut up her womb, how she was embarrassed, how she cried to God, how she wept, how she could not eat or drink, how she made a vow to God. She said, "O God, if only You will give me a son, I will give him back to You as a freewill offering" (see I Samuel 1:11). While she was praying, Eli the priest noticed that her lips were moving. But being old and dim in his eyes, he could only see very vaguely; so he thought Hannah must be drunk. What a judge! But Hannah said, "I am not that kind of woman. I am a woman crying before the Lord" (see I Samuel 1:15-16). Then Eli said, "God has heard you." Immediately, she went back, ate and drank, worshiped God, and returned home.

What is worship? Worship comes through faith. Hannah prayed, asking God for a son. But even before she received a son, she believed in God and, because of her faith in God, she could worship. Very often, we have to wait until our prayer is answered, then we worship God. Before the prayer is answered, we are waiting to see if God is dependable, if He is to be worshiped. We have to wait until the thing is accomplished and then we worship. But if you have faith, you can worship even before the answer comes because you know He has answered. The answer is on the way, so why not worship Him first? That will speed up the answer.

David

David was a worshiper. In II Samuel we read how David sinned and the disciplining hand of God was upon him. God smote the child that was born out of that sin. David fasted and lay on the ground hoping that God would look upon his affliction and be merciful to the child; but the child died. The servants feared to tell him because they said, "Behold, while the child was yet alive, we spoke to him, and he would not hearken to our voice; and how shall we say to him, The child is dead? he may do some harm. But David saw that his servants whispered, and David perceived that the child was dead; and David said to his servants, Is the child dead? And they said, He is dead. Then David arose from the earth, and washed, and anointed himself, and changed his clothing, and entered into the house of Jehovah and worshiped" (II Samuel 12:18b-20a). Isn't this strange? God did not answer his prayer, yet he worshiped God. Why? David knew God. He prayed, hoping that God would be merciful, but when he realized that discipline was necessary, he accepted it and, because he did, he worshiped God.

Oftentimes, we cannot accept discipline; therefore, we will not worship. How can you kiss the hand that strikes you? But if you know whose hand it is that smites you, you can even worship that One. The reason there is so little worship today is because we know so little of discipline. When we are disciplined, we rebel. We refuse to accept it; we murmur. But if we see the love behind discipline, we can worship as David did.

As you read on, you will find the discipline continues in David's house. Even his own son Absalom rebelled against him. He was able to stir up the whole nation, as it were, to rebel against David. David had to flee for his life, and as he was doing so, he climbed to the summit of the Mount of Olives and "worshiped God." He worshiped God when he was fleeing for his life, when his own son wanted his life. He worshiped God when he seemed to have lost everything, even his nation (see II Samuel 15). David knew worship; he was a true worshiper of God.

Of course, we all know that David was the sweet singer of Israel and, of the collection of 150 Psalms, most of them were written by him. As you read them, you find a worshiping spirit there. Oh, how David worshiped God on all occasions! He worshiped God when he was in trouble; he worshiped God when he was in prosperity. And not only did he worship God, but he called the heavens and earth to join with him in this worship because he considered God as worthy. David worshiped God.

There are many other examples of worship in the Old Testament. They worshiped God under all kinds of circumstances, even though they were under the law. The Jews worshiped in Jerusalem in the temple three times a year, and the Samaritans had their own tradition and worshiped on Mt. Gerizim. Yet, even in the Old Testament times when people were really drawn into true worship, they worshiped in spirit and truth. It was based upon their knowledge of God. When you see God, you worship Him.

Examples of Worship in the New Testament

But do not make the mistake of thinking that worship belongs to the Old Testament. Often, when people today try to worship, they go back to the Old Testament as if worship belonged to the Old Testament and you do not find it in the New Testament. But thank God, "The hour is coming and now is when the true worshipers shall worship the Father in spirit and truth" (see John 4:23). Today, we are in a much better position in the matter of worship than the people in the Old Testament times. Therefore, how much more should we know how to worship. With them, the revelation of God was limited, but with us, it is unlimited. They knew God only as God, but we know God as our Father. They knew God transcendent, but we know God imminent. We have a relationship with God our Father that they did not have, so under the New Testament, we ought to worship God much more and much better than the old Testament saints. We should not in any way be behind them.

The Wise Men

As we look to the New Testament, we will find it is full of worship. You remember when Christ was born, the Magi, the wise men, saw the star and traveled from afar. It took them almost two years to arrive at Jerusalem. They inquired saying, "Where is the King of the Jews? We saw His star." They were directed by prophecy and then by the star to that house in Bethlehem. It was no longer the manger because two years had passed, and Joseph and Mary lived in a house with their firstborn. The wise men entered into the house, they saw the Child, and they worshiped Him. They did not worship the mother nor the father; they worshiped the Child. As they worshiped the Child, they offered gold, frankincense, and myrrh (see Matthew 2:7-11). Worship comes through revelation. If there is no revelation, there can be no worship. If the wise men had not seen the star, they would not have been able to come and worship the Child. If we do not have revelation from above to see Him as the Christ, the Son of the living God, how can we worship?

But even when the wise men worshiped the Child, they did not worship just with a physical posture; they worshiped with offerings. They offered something worthy to the Child. They offered gold, frankincense, and myrrh. These were precious things in the eyes of men, yet they offered them to the Lord. Some people say gold speaks of the divine nature of God. Yes, the Child is the Son that is given. Frankincense speaks of the life of our Lord Jesus while on earth—like a sweet savor of frank incense. The incense is so frank it goes out. That is the life of our Lord. Myrrh speaks of the death of the Lord. It is bitter, yet it has healing power. And, of course, Joseph would need some gold because they had to flee to Egypt and stay there.

The wise men came to worship through revelation, and they worshiped with offerings. What is worship? We worship because we know Him, but we are not just to worship with empty words. Offer something to Him; bring your offerings to Him. This is called the sacrifice of praise. When we praise Him, there is a sacrifice there—something that we have gone through, something that we have experienced of Him. We bring these back to Him. "We are being built together a spiritual house, a holy priesthood, to offer up spiritual sacrifices acceptable to God through Jesus Christ" (see I Peter 2:5). As we worship, we offer. Even when we offer praises, they are not just words; it is a sacrifice. In other words, it costs you something. We offer back to Him that which He has given to us: His divinity, His pure life, His resurrection, His glory, His coming. We offer something to Him. Never come to worship with empty hands. Worship surrounded the birth of our Lord.

Simeon

When our Lord Jesus was eight days old, He was presented to the temple and Simeon came. He received him into his arms, blessed God, and said, "Lord, now thou lettest thy bondman go, according to thy word, in peace; for mine eyes have seen thy salvation" (Luke 2:28-30). Even though the word worship is not used here, you know it is worship.

What is worship? It is: treasure the Son. Simeon's whole life on earth was lived for one purpose—to see the salvation of the Lord. When he saw the Savior, he said, "I am ready to go; there is no more desire in me." That is worship.

Do we have such a worshiping spirit? Are we desiring so many things that even when we have Him in our hands, we are not satisfied? Do we really live for Him and Him alone? That is worship.

Mary, the Mother of Jesus

Let's look at Mary, the mother of Jesus. Mary went to visit Elizabeth, and the Bible says, "And it came to pass, as Elizabeth heard the salutation of Mary, the babe leaped in her womb; and Elizabeth was filled with the Holy Spirit, and cried out with a loud voice and said, Blessed art thou amongst women" (Luke 1:41-42). "Mary said, My soul magnifies the Lord, and my spirit has rejoiced in God my Savior" (Luke 1:46-47). She worshiped the Lord, and worship began in her spirit. She said, "My spirit has rejoiced in God my Savior," and then, "My soul magnifies the Lord." Now this is important. Worship does not originate from the soul; it originates in the spirit. It is in your spirit that you have something revealed of Him, and when you see Him in your spirit and have rejoiced in Him in your spirit, then your soul takes this up and magnifies the Lord. How do we magnify the Lord? It is by praises, by singing, by prayer. But when you express these with your emotion, your mind, or your will, it has to begin in your spirit. That is worship.

It is true that Mary was the most blessed among women, favored by God. Yet, on the other hand, it cost her everything. Her praises were sacrifices of praise. When she magnified the Lord and rejoiced in the Lord, it cost her everything. That is worship. If worship does not cost you something, it is very shallow, very superficial. The more it costs you the deeper will be your worship because you see more of His worthiness.

The Life of Our Lord Jesus

As we come to the life of our Lord Jesus, we see that His whole life is characterized by worship. It comes out in many forms. Look at His prayer life. It is worship because He shows us how He depends upon the Father, how He seeks the will of the Father—Not My will but Your will be done (see Matthew 26:39). It comes out in the form of praises. We read in Matthew 11 how He labored in Capernaum, Chorazin, and Bethsaida, yet the people did not receive Him. At the point of disappointment, He turned to God and said, "I praise thee, Father, Lord of the heaven and of the earth, that thou hast hid these things from the wise and prudent, and hast revealed them to babes. Yea, Father, for thus has it been well-pleasing in thy sight" (Matthew 11:25-26). We want our work to be successful, we want our labor to be rewarded, and when these things do not happen, we murmur. We say, "Why?" But our Lord Jesus thanked God. He said, "God, this is your will. I thank You. I am happy. I rejoice in it." This is worship.

When our Lord Jesus offered His life as a sacrifice on the tree, that was the consummation of worship. In Psalm 40 it says:

Sacrifice and oblation thou didst not desire: ears hast thou prepared me. Burnt-offering and sin-offering has thou not demanded; Then said I, Behold, I come, in the volume of the book it is written of me. To do thy good pleasure, my God, is my delight, and thy law is within my heart (vv. 6-8).

The whole life of our Lord Jesus is worship. His life is worship; His death is worship; everything about Him is worship because His whole life is exalting God, honoring the Father, glorifying the Father. That is worship.

Our Lord Jesus not only sets before us an example of worship, but He teaches us much about worship. When He was tempted in the wilderness, the tempter came and showed Him all the kingdoms of the world and said, "All these things will I give thee if, falling down, thou wilt do me homage" (Matthew 4:9). Do you think the devil will give all the kingdoms to you without a string attached? In the first place, the world does not belong to him; he usurped it. In the second place, when he wants to give the world to you, he wants your soul as an exchange. But when he gets your soul, he gets his world back and you get nothing. You lose your soul. "What does it profit a man if he should gain the whole world and lose his soul?" (Mark 8:36). When the tempter tempted our Lord, the Lord said, "Satan, it is written, thou shall worship the Lord your God alone and Him shall ye serve." (Matthew 4:10). The Lord teaches us very clearly that there is only One to be worshiped and that is God, our Father. He is the only One that we must serve.

In John 4, He said we worship the Father in spirit and truth. In Matthew 15, the Lord said to the Pharisees: "This people honor me with the lips, but their heart is far away from me; but in vain do they worship me, teaching as teachings commandments of men" (vv. 8-9). The Lord tells us what worship is not. Worship is not lip service; it must come from the heart. If the heart is there, then the words will be accepted. If the heart is far away from God, then whatever is said is in vain. It must be in spirit, and worship must also be in truth. That is the commandment of God, not the teaching of men. If we worship according to the teaching of men, it is worship in vain, but if we worship according to the commandment of God, keeping the commandment of God, that is worship in truth.

The Leper Who Returned to Give Thanks

In Luke 17, our Lord Jesus healed ten lepers. Only one returned to give thanks. The Lord said, "Did I not heal ten people? Where are the nine? Only this stranger, a Samaritan, returned to give thanks to God." In other words, our Lord is looking for worship. What is worship? Worship is to return and give thanks. Do we ever receive healings, blessings from the Lord and just go away? Do we ever return? Worship is to return and give thanks to God.

The Leper Who Believed and Worshiped

In Matthew 8, the leper came and said, "Lord, if thou wilt, thou art able to cleanse me" (v.2b). Why did he worship? He worshiped because he believed that the Lord was not only able but He was willing. If we believe, we can worship.

The Ruler's Daughter

Then in Matthew 9, the ruler's daughter was dying and he came and worshiped the Lord saying, "My daughter is dying, but come, You can heal her" (see v. 18). Again, worship was based on faith. If you believe, you can worship.

The Disciples in the Ship

In Matthew 14, it says, "The Lord compelled the disciples to go on board ship, and to go on before him to the other side" (see v.22). As they were in the ship, a storm came up in the middle of the sea. The Lord came to them, walking on the water. He calmed the wind, and when those in the ship saw this, they worshiped him. Revelation! When you see, then you will worship.

The Canaanitish Woman

Also in Matthew, we find the Canaanitish woman who came to the Lord and said, "Son of David, have mercy on me" (see Matthew 15:22b). The Lord did not answer her. When the Lord entered into the house, she came forward and the Lord said, "It is not good to give the bread to dogs" (see v.26). (Remember, the dogs here are not wild dogs; they are pet dogs.) So the woman took the lower position and said, "Yes, I am but a pet dog; but a pet dog does have the scraps under the table" (v.27). She worshiped the Lord because of her faith in God.

Mary, Sister of Martha

Then, there is Mary the sister of Martha. Even though the word worship is not used in John 12, you do find worship. When our Lord was sitting at the table with Lazarus, and Martha was busy as usual preparing the food, Mary came with an alabaster flask of pure nard. She broke the neck of the flask and poured the ointment on the Lord, and the fragrance filled the house. That is worship. There was no speech, but there was worship because, to Mary, the Lord was worthy. She saw the worthiness of the Lord, and she was willing to give the very best and the very last to the Lord. That is worship.

Paul

In the epistles, there is also worship. Take Paul as an illustration. He knew how to worship. How do we know? Sometimes, in the midst of his writing, worship breaks forth. Now we say the letter to the Romans is a treatise, a dissertation, because Paul gives the whole range of the salvation of the Lord. When you are writing a dissertation, it may be a mental exercise, but while Paul was writing, he broke forth into worship time and again. For example, look at Romans 9:5 where he is talking about the privileges of the children of Israel: "Whose are the fathers; and of whom, as according to flesh, is the Christ, who is over all, God blessed forever. Amen." Now that is not a dissertation; that is praise. It is worship. When he thought of what God had given to the children of Israel, when he thought of Christ, he could not contain himself. He said this Christ is God above all, blessed forever, Amen! The worship just came forth.

In Romans 11, he is talking about the mercy, the grace, the compassion God has given to us. "O depth of riches both of the wisdom and knowledge of God! how unsearchable his judgments, and untraceable his ways! For who has known the mind of the Lord, or who has been his counselor? or who has first given to him, and it shall be rendered to him? For of him, and through him, and for him are all things: to him be glory for ever. Amen" (vv.33-36). This is worship. It is not just discussion and arguments. There is that worshiping spirit in Paul.

You will find the same thing in chapter 16 as he concludes: "The only wise God, through Jesus Christ, to whom be glory for ever. Amen" (v.27). The apostle Paul does have a spirit of worship.

Worship is a Spirit

Worship is more than just some form or some expressions at some times at some places. Worship is a spirit because we are worshipers. Being a worshiper means that this is what you are. You do not just worship once in a while on certain occasions or in certain places or at certain times. No! To be a worshiper means that is what you are. But how can we be worshipers unless we have the spirit of worship? The spirit of worship is always there; therefore, it should break out at every occasion. There is no limit.

The whole book of Revelation is a book of worship. Someone has said that God created man as a worshiper, and He has been working through the sixty-six books in the Bible until He came to the last book. There, in the book of Revelation, you will find worship. God is surrounded with worshipers. They shall see Him; they shall worship Him; they shall serve Him; they shall have His name upon their foreheads.

We are called to worship. And what is worship? It is impossible to define. We only know that worship is the spontaneous response of those redeemed created ones to the Creator, our Redeemer. Worship is because we see Him through revelation. Worship is to abase ourselves and to exalt Him. Worship is spiritual in nature. It involves our whole being and not just a part. Worship is all-inclusive. It is our very life. Worship is service. It is our work. Worship is that which the Father is seeking, and worship is that which we can give. Someone has said that when you pray, you ask; when you worship, you give. We ask all the time, but how often do we give? God does not require anything from you. If we say we are to repay what He has given to us, we do not know what grace is. We can never repay, but there is one thing that God does look for in us and that is to appreciate Him. All He wants is our appreciation—to give back to Him that which He has given to us, in gratitude, in love. Worship is disinterest. If we are interested in ourselves, we cannot worship; we will not worship, but when we become disinterested in ourselves and interested in Him, then we begin to worship. So dear brothers and sisters, remember that the Father is seeking for worshipers—true worshipers, those who worship Him in spirit and truth.

3—Personal and Corporate Worship

Psalm 95:6,7a—Come, let us worship and bow down; let us kneel before Jehovah our Maker. For he is our God; and we are the people of his pasture and the sheep of his hand.

Acts 2:42—And they persevered in the teaching and fellowship of the apostles, in breaking of bread and prayers.

Revelation 7:9-12—After these things I saw, and lo, a great crowd, which no one could number, out of every nation and tribes and peoples and tongues, standing before the throne, and before the Lamb, clothed with white robes, and palm branches in their hands. And they cry with a loud voice, saying, Salvation to our God who sits upon the throne, and to the Lamb. And all the angels stood around the throne, and the elders, and the four living creatures, and fell before the throne upon their faces, and worshiped God, saying, Amen: Blessing, and glory, and wisdom, and thanksgiving, and honour, and power, and strength, to our God, to the ages of ages. Amen.

Personal Worship

We are considering this matter of worship, and now we will look at the difference between personal and corporate worship. Worship is personal, very personal, because it is based on an intimate relationship. If we do not have a relationship with God our Father, we cannot worship, and no one else may worship for us. It is our spiritual exercise; therefore, it must be very personal. As God is revealed to us in His Son by the Holy Spirit, we begin to worship. So worship is based on our personal relationship and experience with God. It is a personal response of our total being to God. In the Bible, you will find Abraham worshiped, also Jacob, Moses, Gideon, Hannah, Samuel, and many others. It was very personal. Every one of us must have a personal relationship with God in such a way that it comes forth as worship. We are worshipers, and a worshiper should worship. Therefore, our whole life ought to be a worship unto God.

In our personal worship, I believe it is good to begin our day with worship. In the Old Testament times, in the early morning in the temple, they burned a burnt-offering unto God. This offering was slowly consumed by the fire throughout the day. It was not burned up in an hour. Towards the end of the day, as the morning offering was consumed, they had to offer another burnt-offering. This evening offering was so that the sacrifice might burn through the night. The burnt-offering on the altar was never absent. It was always there. It was a continual offering unto God; we know a burnt-offering was a sign or token of worship. Our Lord Jesus offered himself as a burnt-offering unto the Father to satisfy the heart of the Father and, in union with our Lord Jesus, we offer ourselves in Christ as a burnt-offering to God. It is our worship to Him, and this ought to be continued day and night. It is a spirit of worship.

Again, I will emphasize that worship is not something which we do only at a certain hour or in a certain place. Worship is a spirit; therefore, we must have that worshiping spirit throughout the day and night. It should always be with us. So I believe it is a good thing when we begin the day with worship.

Why do we emphasize that every believer should have a morning watch, spending a little time with the Lord early in the morning before you do anything? Why is this so essential to our Christian life? It is because we want to begin our day with the Lord. And we do this by worshiping Him. I do not know how you begin your day with the Lord. Do you just go to Him and ask for this and that for the day, rushing into the presence of the Lord, making your petitions known to Him? Or do you go to the Lord and, in quietness, pour out your spirit to Him in love, in worship, in adoration? I do believe it would be a real help if, even before we pray, that is, asking for anything, we would be very quiet before Him. If we open our hearts towards Him and behold His beauty, gazing upon Him in our spirit, just a minute or two, this will help cultivate that spirit of worship that we need throughout the day.

Also, it is always good if, when you have a little time during the day while you are working or whatever you may be doing, you will just stop for a few seconds and lift up your eyes, lift up your heart to the Lord and just say, "Lord, I worship You, I adore You, I love You." In one sense, we may say this is practicing the presence of the Lord. You remember the little book by Brother Lawrence called *The Practice of the Presence of God,* which is a classic. Brother Lawrence was a cook in a monastery. He cultivated the holy habit of always being in the presence of the Lord even while he was busy in the kitchen with all the noises around him. In the midst of all this, he would lift his spirit up and commune with God.

I do believe it is good practice throughout the day to just take a few seconds and lift up your heart and worship Him, keeping yourself in the spirit of worship. If you are doing this, whenever there is a blessing from the Lord, immediately you will turn to Him and give thanks. You will not forget to return and thank Him for what He has done for you. Or sometimes, when you have problems, oppositions, persecutions, or the Lord has taken something from you, instead of murmuring, turn to Him and say, "Blessed be the name of the Lord. It is He who gives. It is He who takes away" (see Job 1:21b). We need to have a spirit of worship within us. If we do not, then when such times come, no doubt you will murmur. You are not ready to worship God. You do not see Him and, if you do not see Him, you cannot worship Him. So I do believe it is a good thing, knowing that worship is a spirit, to cultivate personally, individually this spirit of worship. We do not need to dwell too much on personal worship because this is something that every one of us ought to do because we are called to be worshipers.

Corporate Worship

In the Scripture, you will find there is another kind of worship which is corporate worship. We are not alone. We are members of one body; we belong to one family; we are a new nation. Therefore, our worship cannot just be limited to the personal level. It has to be raised to the corporate level.

So far as the nature of worship is concerned, there is no difference between the personal and the corporate; that is to say, worship is worship. But when you come to practice, corporate worship is somewhat different from personal worship. Before we go into that, we will look into some things concerning the children of Israel.

The Children of Israel

Israel was a nation before God, and in Exodus, they were told by God that all the males must go to Jerusalem three times a year to offer sacrifices and worship God. You can just imagine the Jews traveling from all the different cities of the world, bringing their families to Jerusalem. When they did this, no doubt, the crowd increased in number when they met others on the way. While they were traveling, we are told they usually sang Psalms together until they came to

Jerusalem. After they arrived, not only did every family offer sacrifices and eat together, but sacrifices would also be offered for the whole nation as all came together to the temple. They would pray together, live in booths, keep the feasts, and listen to the word of God and have it explained to them together. They were a people, a nation; therefore, they worshiped God together as a nation.

When David brought the ark to the city of David, we are told that he gathered the people together because it was a corporate matter. It was not just David alone but the whole nation was to be rightly related with the ark of God, that is, with God. They worshiped as one people.

When Solomon dedicated the temple, he did the same thing. He gathered all the people together, and there, they worshiped God as one people.

In Kings and Chronicles, whenever there was a revival or a return to God in the nation, the king would bring all the people together to worship. For instance, in II Chronicles 20, King Jehoshaphat and the children of Israel were faced with a crisis. The armies of Moab and Ammon came to fight against them, and Jehoshaphat knew that he could not meet with that great army, so he gathered the people. They fasted together, they waited upon the Lord, and then this word from the Lord came to them: "Ye shall not have to fight on this occasion: set yourselves, stand and see the salvation of Jehovah who is with you!" (II Chronicles 20:17). When this prophecy came to them, not only did the king bow down with his face to the ground, but all the people bowed down, worshiped, and sang praises unto God. They worshiped as one people.

In II Chronicles 29, there was a great revival among the children of Israel during the reign of Hezekiah. The temple of God was cleansed, and King Hezekiah gathered all the people together. They worshiped God with the singers singing according to the commandment of David. Again, they worshiped God as one people.

In Ezra, when the remnant returned from the Babylonian captivity, they laid the foundation of the house. The people were weeping and shouting, and the priests were blowing the trumpets and sounding the cymbals. They worshiped as one man.

In Nehemiah, you will find the same thing. Nehemiah gathered the people together, and when Ezra the priest stood up and read the book, all the people stood up, bowed down, and worshiped God.

If this was true with the children of Israel, how much more should it be so with us today. They were just a nation, but we are a family, a body. Our relationship is a closer one than that of the children of Israel.

The Church

We do find in the Bible such a thing called corporate worship. In fact, our personal worship is the foundation of our corporate worship; therefore, if, during the day and the week in our personal lives, we do not worship, when we come together, there is no way for us to worship. If our personal worship is strong, our corporate worship will be strong. If our personal worship is very much lacking, then our corporate worship will be very poor. It is the foundation of corporate worship.

In the New Testament, our Lord Jesus and His disciples were one family, and that is the reason they had the last Passover together. The disciples did not go to their different homes. During the Passover Feast every family would gather together and eat the Passover Lamb. Here our Lord Jesus gathered His own as one family and kept the Passover Feast. It was during this time that He broke the bread, passed the cup and said, "This do in remembrance of me" (Luke 22:19b). He also conversed with them, telling them many things which were upon His heart and, finally, He went to the Father and prayed for them. At the very last, they sang a hymn and went to the garden of Gethsemane, where our Lord Jesus went to the presence of the Father in prayer. The whole atmosphere was one of worship.

On the day of Pentecost, when Peter stood up, the eleven stood with him. Why? On that day, the Holy Spirit did something. When the Holy Spirit came down, and they were all baptized in one Spirit, the 120 individuals became a body of 120 members. They were more than individual believers; they were then a body of 120 members, so when Peter stood up, the eleven stood with him. Even on that day when the 3,000 came to the Lord, despite that great number being added to them, they *all* persevered, *all* continued—3,120— in the teaching and the fellowship of the apostles, in the breaking of bread, and in prayer (Acts 2:42).

What is the teaching of the apostles? It is none other than the teaching of Christ. What is the fellowship of the apostles? It is the fellowship of Christ. The teaching is on the truth side; the fellowship is on the experience side. You have the objective truth; you have the subjective experience—the whole Christian life. But why is the breaking of bread and prayer especially mentioned? It is because the breaking of bread and prayer are more than just remembrance and petition. It is true that the breaking of bread is remembrance because the Lord Jesus said, "Do this in remembrance of me." But it is also more than remembrance; it is corporate worship.

Praying together is more than just asking or intercession. Prayer is worship. You remember how our Lord Jesus taught the disciples to pray, what we often call the Lord's prayer, but actually it is the church's prayer. The Lord said, "Our Father ..." It is corporate. "Our Father who art in the heavens, let thy name be sanctified, let thy kingdom come, let thy will be done as in heaven so upon the earth" (Matthew 6:9-10). What is this? It is worship. The church's prayer begins with worship and, in that worshiping spirit, it comes down to: "Give us this day our daily bread. And forgive us our debts, as we forgive our debtors. And lead us not into temptation, but deliver us from evil: For thine is the kingdom, and the power, and the glory, for ever. Amen" (Matthew 6:11-13 KJV). This is worship. This prayer which the Lord has taught us begins and ends with worship. Therefore, we see that from the early church up to our present time, the church is a worshiping church.

In I Peter 2:5, it says that as we come to the Lord, we "as living stones, are being built up a spiritual house, a holy priesthood, to offer spiritual sacrifices acceptable to God by Jesus Christ." In the Old Testament times, the children of Israel went to the temple in Jerusalem to offer burnt offerings, peace offerings, and other sacrifices, but where is the temple today? We are the temple. As living stones we are built up together a spiritual house. We are the temple of God, and a temple is a place of worship. So when God's people come together, it is for one reason—to worship God. How do we worship? We worship as a holy priesthood, not just individual priests each doing whatever he would like. In other words, we worship God as one unit under the direction of the High Priest. Everyone has their part, but it is a holy priesthood to offer spiritual sacrifices acceptable to God through Jesus Christ—not with sheep, not with cattle, not with doves but with spiritual sacrifices. What are these spiritual sacrifices?

It is the Christ who has been revealed and given to each one of us through the week. We just bring back to God the Christ that He has given. It can come forth in praises, in prayers, in songs, in words, but it is Christ being offered back to God. How that satisfies God's heart! So we not only worship individually, we worship together. And there are times when the church should gather and worship Him together as a family, as a body. This is corporate worship.

Differences Between Personal and Corporate Worship

There are some differences between personal and corporate worship. There is not any difference in nature; it is only in practice. Corporate worship requires more spiritual understanding, more self-control or discipline than personal worship. In corporate worship there is another dimension or relationship added. Our personal worship is a vertical relationship—you and God, you and Christ. This is the height and depth of worship. You pour out your heart in love towards

God, and He gives himself to you without measure. The more revelation of Him you receive, the richer, the deeper will be your worship.

However, when you come to corporate worship, there is also a horizontal relationship. This is the width and length of worship. It is not only between you and the Lord, but now your brothers and sisters with you. And because of this added dimension, it requires more understanding and more discipline.

Paul said in II Corinthians 5:13: "I am beside myself towards God; but I am sober towards you." In other words, when he is alone with God, he can be beside himself. It seems as if he can do anything he wants, of course, in the right way because God understands. You can roll before Him; you can leap before Him; you can crawl before Him; you can cry before Him. You can do anything because it is before Him. Oh, how He understands. When you come to the presence of God, you do not need to pretend; you do not need to try very hard. Just be yourself. Paul said that before God he could be beside himself, but towards the brothers and sisters he was sober. In other words, he exercised self-control when he was with the brothers and sisters because they may not always understand. On the contrary, they may very easily misunderstand or even be stumbled. They could be offended, so for their sake you have to exercise restraint.

There is an interesting case in the Old Testament when David brought the ark to the city of David. He danced before the ark. Oh, he was beside himself when he thought of the mercy and the grace of God that had come upon him to take him out of the sheepfold and make him the king over God's people. When he thought of what the Lord had done for him, his love for the Lord was so great that when he saw the ark, he was just beside himself. He forgot himself. He danced before the Lord, and he did not dance mildly. I think he danced very wildly because he uncovered himself, and his wife Michal, looking out from the window and seeing the king doing that, despised him from her heart. When David came and blessed the family, she said, "O the king has uncovered himself today in the eyes of the handmaids of his servants. How shameful it is." But David said, "Oh no, I played before the Lord, and I want to make myself yet more vile than thus." David's spirit was right. He played before the Lord. He was humble before the Lord, not as the king, but very humble, and he wanted to humble himself more before the Lord. His spirit was right, and God blessed him. Michal's spirit was wrong and God shut up her womb (see II Samuel 6:14,16,20-23). Now, this is true; but I want to use it in another sense. David played before God, and there was not anything wrong, but in the presence of the people, Michal was stumbled. Brothers and sisters, you may play before the Lord, but do not stumble your brothers and sisters.

Principles of Corporate Worship

There is a difference between personal and corporate worship. Corporate worship requires more under-standing and more discipline. In I Corinthians 14, the apostle Paul instructs the church in Corinth on how to meet. Of course, the type of meeting in this chapter is called a fellowship meeting because it is the time when the spiritual gifts are being exercised. It is a time when the brothers and sisters are gathered together, and everyone just offers what gift or gifts the Lord has given to each for the building up of the body of Christ. The apostle Paul gives them certain directions, and I believe these principles are applicable to the time when we come together to worship because spiritual principles apply to all kinds of public meetings. So even though it is especially directed to fellowship meetings, I believe it will help us to know how to worship together. There are three things which we would like to mention.

In Mind Be Grown-Up

"Brethren, be not children in your minds, but in malice be babes; but in your minds be grown men" (I Corinthians 14:20). The Bible teaches that we should be like little children. The Lord said, "Unless ye are converted and become as little children, ye will not at all enter into the kingdom of the heavens" (Matthew 18:3). Who is the greatest in the kingdom of heaven? Those who are like little children because the will of God is hidden from the wise and the prudent but is revealed to babes (see Matthew 11:25). When we come to this matter of faith, we ought to be childlike. The more childlike you are in faith, the better you are. Often, the reason we do not have faith is that we are too wise and too prudent. Be childlike in faith but in mind be grown-up. Do you see the difference?

What is the mind of a grown-up? The mind of a grown-up ought not to be just thinking of himself but thinking of others. The mind of a child thinks only of himself. I think some parents experience this. The babies think only of themselves. If they feel hungry, they cry, whether it is midnight or not. They do not care what you think; they only know what they want. The mind of a child is self-centered, but the mind of a grown-up should always think in terms of other people. If a person is self-centered always thinking of himself, then he never grows up. He may be fifty years old, or he may be sixty-five, but he has never grown up. The mind of a grown-up is that he thinks of the well-being of other people. Now this is important in corporate worship.

Also, in corporate worship, we should not be so conscious of our brothers and sisters as to whether they approve or disapprove. Forget yourself and concentrate on Him. Now that is right, but what do we mean by this? You should not be so conscious of your brothers and sisters as to whether they will approve or disapprove, but at the same time consider them. Now that is a great difference. To be conscious of them in terms of approval or disapproval will paralyze you, but considering your brothers and sisters is the mind of a grown-up. Will that which I am doing build up the body, or will it just be myself? We do not come just to enjoy ourselves; we come to enjoy the Lord and one another.

Paul spent 25 verses in chapter 14 just on this point. Verses 1-25 are centered upon this matter: "In mind be grown-up." He discovered that in the church at Corinth they were, in mind, still babes. When they came together, they were so anxious to enjoy themselves that they forgot to build up the body, so Paul used two gifts to illustrate this. One was the gift of tongues, and the other one was the gift of prophecy. He said that when God's people are together in the meeting, prophecy is far superior than tongues because tongues edify you but prophecy edifies others. Now that is the mind of a grown-up. Unless a tongue is interpreted, you are being edified yourself. Thank God for that, but you do not edify other people. Therefore, prophecy is superior to tongues in the meeting.

Paul also said that if you speak in tongues and it is not interpreted, no one can say "Amen" with you because they do not know what you are saying. In the corporate meeting, how important it is that brothers and sisters join in with you. If you are praising the Lord, let the other brothers and sisters join in with you. If you are praising the Lord alone—though in public—and the brothers and sisters do not understand, they cannot join in and say, "Amen." It becomes personal worship; it is no longer corporate worship. That is why prophecy is better than tongues in a meeting.

If therefore the whole assembly come together in one place, and all speak with tongues, and simple persons enter in, or unbelievers, will not they say ye are mad? But if all prophesy, and some unbeliever or simple person come in, he is convicted of all, he is judged of all; the secrets of his heart are manifested; and thus, falling upon his face, he will do homage to God, reporting that God is indeed amongst you (I Corinthians 14:23-25).

Do you see the difference? First of all, in corporate worship, we need to develop the mind of a grown-up. Do not come together just to enjoy yourself. We come together to let the Lord enjoy us and to enjoy one another. In mind be grown-up. This is the first thing.

Each Has Something to Bring

What is it then, brethren? Whenever ye come together, each of you has a psalm, has a teaching, has a tongue, has a revelation, has an interpretation. Let all things be done to edification (I Corinthians 14:26).

When God's people come together as a corporate body to worship, remember one thing: You must not come empty-handed. Whenever the children of Israel appeared before God to worship in the temple in Jerusalem, they all brought their baskets and cattle with them. No one came to worship God empty-handed. They did not need to come empty-handed because there was plenty. They were in the promised land—a land flowing with milk and honey. They were in a land that was blessed by God. God would open the heaven and give them rain and dew so they would have plenty in the land unless they were unfaithful to God or they were lazy. If they were unfaithful to God, He would shut up the heaven. If they were lazy and did not work in the field, of course, they would be poor. But being a people of

God, under God's open heaven, each doing their own duty, then every one of them could come with full baskets to worship God. No one came empty-handed.

Applying this to us today, when we come together, the Bible says, "each has ..." In other words, before you come, each one has something to bring. You do not have to come empty-handed. Now, isn't it terrible if, when we come together on the Lord's Day to worship, no one prepares, no one brings anything, no one goes to the Lord beforehand and asks Him to bless us with something that we can bring back to Him as our worship? Suppose no one prepares, no one works, no one has anything, and we just come together and sit there hoping that God will have plenty. A time of worship is not the time to ask God to give. It is the time that we give to Him. If we do not bring anything, then what do we have to give to Him? Nothing! This is important.

During the week is the time when we live under an open heaven. It is the time that we commune with

God, the time that we are faithful to Him, the time that we diligently till our ground and diligently seek Him. If we live such a life during the week, then when we come together, we all have our hands full. One may have a hymn; the other may have a teaching; the other may have a tongue; the other may have an interpretation; the other may have a revelation. In other words, what we have is varied and different, but we all have something. Everyone, "each has …" If each has and we come with our hands full, how rich will be our time together and how much God's heart will be satisfied. The problem is we are either lazy during the week or we are unfaithful, and the heaven is like brass over us. When we come, we come with empty hands. We want to be filled by others.

It is the responsibility of every brother and sister. It is not just for a few to bear the whole burden before the Lord and, as it were, try to drag and pull. No! Every brother and sister must come with something prepared. Ask the Lord what it is that He wants you to bring as an expression of worship to Him. You will discover that we will all bring something, and it will probably be varied: some in songs, very poetic, others in teaching, or tongues, or interpretations, or revelations, or whatever it may be. Everyone needs to bring something. This is an important part of worship.

Let Everything Be Done with Order

But let all things be done comelily and with order
(I Corinthians 14:40).

Suppose we all bring something. Our hands are full, and, no doubt, what we bring with us is so varied and different because our God is so rich. But if we dump all this together which we bring, will it be ugliness and disorder? I believe it will.

Suppose, during the week, the Lord shows you His love, and you desire to bring the love of God back to present this to Him. Then maybe another brother has passed through great troubles, and he begins to sympathize with Christ and His sufferings. He is just feeling the sufferings of Christ; so, he comes with that suffering spirit and wants to offer that back to God. Or suppose the Lord has kept another through temptations and trials. As he sees the faithfulness of the Lord, he wants to come and bring them to God. Or perhaps someone experiences the victory of Christ, or someone else experiences the cross or discipline in his life. When we come to worship Him with all these different things, one moment we are going to a house of mourning, and the next moment we are going to a wedding party. It is chaos—great confusion. They all come from the Lord, but let all things be done comelily. *Comelily* means "beautifully, with beauty." Let all things be done harmoniously; let all things be done as a symphony. It is like an orchestra with all its instruments—some are like a violin, some are like a harp, some are like a clarinet or trombone. All these instruments give different sounds, but together, they harmonize; they synchronize.

How can this be? How can it be with order, with no confusion, no jarring notes, no disturbances or distractions but everything just building up to a crescendo? Well, thank God, we have a Conductor who is the Holy Spirit. When we come together with our hands full, ready to offer them, we are all as these musicians sitting at their post with their various instruments and their eyes on the conductor. You just do not come in and start to play. Every eye is on the conductor, and as the baton of the conductor begins to move or his hand begins to move to point to one to come up here and one to go down there, then these instruments are played according to how they are conducted. There is a time for you to come in; there is a time for you to be quiet. This is the Holy Spirit. We believe the Holy Spirit is present, and He is conducting us, guiding us, leading us in worship, in praise, and when He is leading, there is no confusion. Everything will come in just at the right time and will build up until we come to the point where we have to break the bread and drink the cup. We realize we simply have to! Everything is done beautifully and with order. The order here is not prearranged. That would be a program. This order is divinely arranged, and it is for this reason that we need understanding and self-control.

When the Holy Spirit is moving a meeting, there is the Spirit of the meeting there. The Spirit is like the wind. When the wind blows, there is a direction; so when the Spirit is leading us, there will be a direction. It is not confusion. This is where we need to discern the direction of the Holy Spirit. Where does the wind blow? How is the Spirit leading? And as the Spirit leads, we follow; we cooperate. This is understanding.

Suppose the Spirit in the meeting is full of joy and you come in with a groan. There would be no under-standing there. Can you attend a wedding party with a groan? You will spoil the whole atmosphere. We need understanding. And this is the time we need self-control. "And spirits of prophets are subject to prophets" (I Corinthians 14:32). You say, "I have prophecy." All right, you have prophecy, but does it mean that because you have a prophecy that you have to prophesy? Some people say, "I cannot help it. When the spirit of prophecy is upon me, I have to prophesy whether it is midnight or not." No! The spirit of the prophet is subject to the prophet. "And let two or three prophets speak." It is too much. Keep quiet. There is nothing wrong with the prophecy. God has given you that prophecy, but it may not be the right time to share it. In an orchestra, when it should be a very, very quiet time, with a flute being played, if there were a sudden BOOM sound from the bass drum, it would be ugly. When God's people come together, there is much for us to learn. Sometimes we think we are geniuses. We can just come together to meet and worship and serve the Lord, and we know how to do it. There is much we need to learn, especially in the time of worship.

I repeat: How we need to know the mind of the Spirit! How we need to exercise self-control! This is the time that really shows.

Sometimes, when we are talking about these things, people will say, "Well, if it is that difficult, then the cleverest thing is to keep your mouth shut. Do not participate. Just be passive. Then you can never be wrong." Yes, you can never be wrong; but you *are* wrong because this is the time that we should all bring something to the Lord. The Lord Jesus said, "Were not the ten cleansed? but the nine, where are they? There have not been found to return and give glory to God save this stranger" (Luke 17:17,18).

May the Lord help us.

4—The Breaking of Bread

Acts 2:42—And they persevered in the teaching and fellowship of the apostles, in breaking of bread and prayers.

I Corinthians 10:16-22—The cup of blessing which we bless, is it not the communion of the blood of the Christ? The bread which we break, is it not the communion of the body of the Christ? Because we, being many, are one loaf, one body; for we all partake of that one loaf. See Israel according to flesh: are not they who eat the sacrifices in communion with the altar? What then do I say? that what is sacrificed to an idol is anything, or that an idol is anything? But that what the nations sacrifice they sacrifice to demons, and not to God. Now I do not wish you to be in communion with demons. Ye cannot drink the Lord's cup, and the cup of demons: ye cannot partake of the Lord's table, and of the table of demons. Do we provoke the Lord to jealousy? are we stronger than he?

I Corinthians 11:23-33—For I received from the Lord, that which I also delivered to you, that the Lord Jesus, in the night in which he was delivered up, took bread, and having given thanks broke it, and said, This is my body, which is for you:

this do in remembrance of me. In like manner also the cup, after having supped, saying, This cup is the new covenant in my blood: this do, as often as ye shall drink it, in remembrance of me. For as often as ye shall eat this bread, and drink the cup, ye announce the death of the Lord, until he come. So that whosoever shall eat the bread, or drink the cup of the Lord, unworthily, shall be guilty in respect of the body and of the blood of the Lord. But let a man prove himself, and thus eat of the bread, and drink of the cup. For the eater and drinker eats and drinks judgment to himself, not distinguishing the body. On this account many among you are weak and infirm, and a good many are fallen asleep. But if we judged ourselves, so were we not judged. But being judged, we are disciplined of the Lord, that we may not be condemned with the world. So that, my brethren, when ye come together to eat, wait for one another.

We are created as worshipers, and we are redeemed to be true worshipers—those who worship the Father in spirit and truth. The coming of our Lord Jesus and the work He has accomplished on Calvary's cross makes us true worshipers. We do not just worship a God who is transcendent, distant from us. We worship a God who is our Father, who is near us. He is in us, and we are in Him. Worship is our spontaneous, free response—the response of a loving heart towards our God, our Father through our Lord Jesus Christ in the power of the Holy Spirit. Worship is not just an act; it is a life. It is not just we do something with external posture; it is with our heart. It involves our total being so that our whole being will go out to Him to worship, to appreciate, to adore, and to love Him.

The Breaking of Bread

In the early church, the believers continued, persevered in the teaching and fellowship of the apostles, in the breaking of bread and in prayers (see Acts 2:42). What is the teaching of the apostles? Of course, we know that this is none other than the teaching of Christ. They do not have their own teaching apart from Christ. What they teach is what they have been taught—what has been revealed to them by Christ.

The fellowship of the apostles is none other than the fellowship of Christ. Again, we find that the apostles do not have a separate fellowship; it is the fellowship of Christ. The teaching of the apostles gives us the truth—objective truth. The fellowship of the apostles gives us experience—subjective experience. The teaching of the apostles teaches us what Christ has accomplished for us on the cross—the finished work of Christ. The fellowship of the apostles shows us the work of the Holy Spirit in us to bring us into fellowship. So the early believers continued on, persevered in the teaching and the fellowship of the apostles in both the objective truth and the subjective experience, in both the knowledge of the finished work of Christ and the experience of the Holy Spirit working in their lives.

This teaching and the fellowship of the apostles is expressed in a practical way—in the breaking of bread and in prayers. The breaking of bread and prayers are the two basic corporate expressions of the teaching and the fellowship of the apostles. That is the reason great emphasis was put on the breaking of bread and prayers in the early church.

Today, when we say we are going to worship, or we see a sign that says "Worship Service," probably, to most people, it just means an hour set apart on a certain day, mostly on the Lord's Day. There, some songs are sung, some words are read, some prayers are offered and, most important of all, a message is given. In other words, as God's people come to worship, they really come to hear a sermon, a message. That is about all people know of worship. But even though there is a place for the delivering of God's word, preaching as we would call it, the breaking of bread is actually the center of corporate worship. That is why, in the early days, the believers gathered daily with one accord in the temple, and they broke bread from house to house as they ate their meals with gladness (see Acts 2:46b).

I wonder what they did when they gathered in the temple area. They had a tremendous number of believers in Jerusalem at that time because on the day of Pentecost 3,000 were added, and then the Lord added to them daily. There was not a house big enough to contain all of them, so they gathered in the temple area, probably in Solomon's Porch. No doubt, at this time, they must have listened to the apostles relating Christ to them and what He had done for them. But I wonder if, when they gathered in the temple area, it was the time when they really gave themselves to prayer. Prayer was the life of the church in the early days, and it was their expression of worshiping God.

On the other hand, you find they broke bread from house to house. Breaking bread was their expression of corporate worship. As you read on in the book of Acts, in chapter 20, we see that Paul came to Troas and stayed there for seven days. While he was there, the Bible says that they gathered together on the Lord's Day to break bread (v.7). In other words, the reason for their coming together was to break bread.

How different it is today. When God's people come together today, they come to hear a message, a sermon; but in the early days, God's people gathered to break bread because worship was the life of the church. Therefore, it is something for us to really consider before the Lord. I think we have to get our priorities straight. When we gather as God's people, we need to come with a worshiping spirit instead of coming to hear God's word spoken. It is true that there is a place for the ministry of God's word, an important place. On the one hand, it will help us worship, but on the other hand, it is the result of worship.

We must remember that we come together to worship the Lord, and the one way to express our corporate worship in the church is by the breaking of bread. So I do hope that from now on, as we gather on the Lord's Day, that we do not come with the mentality to hear the preaching of the word. Yes, the word must be preached. There is a need for it. But I hope that our mentality will be that we have come to worship the Lord. And worship is expressed by the breaking of the bread. This will be the center of the life of the church.

The breaking of bread has a two-fold meaning. On the one side, it is the Lord's Table, and the emphasis is on communion. On the other, it is the Lord's Supper, and the emphasis is on remembrance—remembering the Lord.

The Lord's Supper—Remembrance

For I received from the Lord, that which I also delivered to you, that the Lord Jesus, in the night in which he was delivered up, took bread, and having given thanks broke it, and said, This is my body, which is for you: this do in remembrance of me. In like manner also the cup, after having supped, saying, This cup is the new covenant in my blood: this do, as often as ye shall drink it, in remembrance of me (I Corinthians 11:23-25).

In I Corinthians 11, we are told that the breaking of bread is to help us remember the Lord. There it is called "the Lord's supper" (v. 20). It is there that we remember Him. We remember what He has done for us, how His blood was shed for us, and His body was broken for us.

Notice that the bread is mentioned first and then the cup. The bread which we break is the body of Christ broken for us. The Lord said, "this do in remembrance of me" (v. 24). After the bread is the cup, which is the cup of the New Covenant sealed by the blood of our Lord Jesus. Again the Lord said, "This do in remembrance of me" (v.25).

The loaf which we break stands for that body which our Lord Jesus took upon himself in His incarnation. In this body, He did all the will of God. In this body, He offered himself as a spotless sacrifice by the eternal Spirit. In this body that is broken for us, He gives life to us. He unites us as one body unto God. So when we come together to break this loaf, we remember how His body was broken for us that we may have life and be united together to God our Father.

As we take this cup, we see how His blood was shed for the remission of our sins, that our sins may be cleansed and forgiven. This blood that cleanses our sin is the very blood that sealed the New Covenant. The cup stands for the New Covenant. God has made a New Covenant with us through the blood—an unbroken covenant. This covenant is described in Hebrews 8:

Giving my laws into their mind, I will write them also upon their hearts; and I will be to them for God, and they shall be to me for people. And they shall not teach each his fellow-citizen, and each his brother, saying, Know the Lord; because all shall know me in themselves, from the little one among them unto the great among them. Because I will be merciful to their unrighteousnesses, and their sins and their lawlessnesses I will never remember anymore (vv. 10b-12).

This is the New Covenant, sealed by the blood of our Lord Jesus. It cannot be broken. This is our portion; this is our inheritance.

So as we come to remember Him, we remember all that He is and what He has done for us. Of course, we cannot help but worship Him. In the breaking of bread, remembrance is worship.

For as often as ye shall eat this bread, and drink the cup, ye announce the death of the Lord, until he come (v.26).

Also, when we are remembering Him, we exhibit His death—we announce His death. We see on the table the loaf and the cup. The blood is separated from the body. This means death. So we are exhibiting the death of our Lord Jesus. In other words, His death is the testimony of the church. We testify to the world—both the seen and the unseen, both good and bad angels—that Christ has died. And since He has died, He has accomplished all that God has sent Him to accomplish. It is done!

At the same time, we are looking forward to His return. It is not just a looking back to remember what He has done for us. It is not only to exhibit His death as a present testimony. But it is also a hope, looking forward to the day when He shall return, and we shall eat and drink with Him in a new way. This is the Lord's Supper, and this is the part of remembrance.

The Lord's Table—Communion

The cup of blessing which we bless, is it not the communion of the blood of the Christ? The bread which we break, is it not the communion of the body of the Christ? Because we, being many, are one loaf, one body; for we all partake of that one loaf (I Corinthians 10:16-17).

In I Corinthians 10, we are told that the breaking of bread is "the Lord's table" (v. 21). When the table is mentioned, we know immediately that it is communion or fellowship. As we eat and drink together at a table, we fellowship together. So the emphasis there is on communion or fellowship.

Communion is represented by this phrase "the Lord's table."

Notice here that the cup comes first: "The cup of blessing which we bless, is it not the communion of the blood of the Christ?" (v. 16a). Then the loaf is mentioned: "The bread which we break, is it not the communion of the body of the Christ?" (v. 16b). Why are they in this order? When you come to the actual experience, without the blood how can we share His life? Blood must be shed. Our sins must be remitted, and then we can receive His life in us. So when you come to communion, you will find the cup comes first and the loaf follows. Now it is a communion, a fellowship with the blood of the Lord and with the life of the Lord. This is not transubstantiation, nor is it just representation. This is a spiritual experience. In other words, when we are drinking the cup and when we are eating the bread, the produce of the vine in the cup does not transform into the physical blood of our Lord Jesus, nor does the loaf transform into the physical body of our Lord who was crucified on Calvary's cross. The produce of the vine remains the produce of the vine; the loaf remains the loaf. Yet in our spirit, as we are partaking of the cup and of the loaf, we are in actual communion with the blood of our Lord Jesus and the life of our Lord Jesus. As we drink this cup, in our spirit we are once again experiencing the cleansing power of the blood of our Lord Jesus. The blood that was shed two thousand years ago becomes a present experience through the Holy Spirit. We are again in touch and experiencing the power of the blood of our Lord Jesus in spiritual reality. So it is more than a representation, more than symbolism. One group of Christians believes in transubstantiation and another group believes in symbolism, but this is neither; it is a spiritual reality.

The same thing is true when we break the bread. Even though it is bread that we take in, yet in our spirit we are in touch with the life of our Lord Jesus. That grain of wheat has fallen into the ground and died, and it has borne much fruit. This life of our Lord Jesus is released through the cross in us. And once again, we experience the resurrection life, the power of His resurrection in our life, and this gives us strength for the week that is ahead of us.

This is a very real communion experience. It is not a ritual. It is a real fellowship; it is a real communion with the blood and the life of our Lord Jesus. After we have drunk the cup and we have taken the loaf, we will go out as a new people, renewed in our spirit by the life of our Lord Jesus. This is the only way that we can live on this earth.

The communion has another aspect. Even though we are many, we are one loaf, one body. Therefore, the communion is not only with Christ, but we commune with those who are Christ's because this loaf represents the whole body of Christ. This loaf includes all God's people, not only those who are meeting together in this room but those believers in all of Richmond. Not only that, it includes the believers in all the world, every brother and sister in the Lord. We are in communion with the whole body. We are not just in communion with a few members. This enlarges our vision, enlarges our heart, and increases our love for the brethren. So this communion is very, very real. After we have taken the loaf, we cannot go out and be exclusive or narrow in our feeling. We have to love our brothers and sisters because this is what the loaf is. So when we come together to commune in such a way, no doubt, it draws out worship. How can we commune with Christ and not see His worthiness and not be stirred into worship? We have to worship. It is natural. He has not only saved us, but He has saved so many brothers and sisters. We have such a large family. We belong to each other, and when we see this, we cannot help but praise and thank Him for what He has done.

Preparation for the Breaking of Bread

Again, I will say the breaking of bread is not a ritual. It is not something that we just do as a habit. The breaking of bread is very real; it is worship, it is remembrance, and it is communion. Since this is so, we

must partake in a worthy manner. When we come together to break the bread, when we come to worship
as a corporate body, we must come in a worthy
manner. It is true, in one sense we are never worthy.
Who is worthy? No one! Only the Lord is worthy. We
are not worthy in ourselves, but He has made us
worthy. He has saved us. He has opened a new and
living way for us (Hebrews 10:20), and that is the
reason we can come. But even so, we must come in a
worthy manner.

Come with a Proper Attitude

First of all, before we come to break the bread, before
we come to worship, what should be our attitude?
You remember the parable of the king in Matthew 22
and Luke 14. The king prepared a marriage feast for
his son and invited many people to come. But at the
time when the feast was ready and he sent his
servants out to tell those invited to come, we find
that they made light of it. They despised it. They
were careless about it. One said, "I have bought five

yoke of oxen and must go and try them." Another said, "I have bought some land and must go and see it." Still another said, "I have just married and I cannot leave my wife" (see Luke 14:18-20). They all made excuses and would not come. In other words, they despised it.

Before we come to break the bread, we must not make light of it; we must not be careless. In other words, we do not just come in a careless way; that is, since it is our habit to meet together on the Lord's Day, therefore, when the time comes, we just come, and there is no preparation beforehand.

Or some people despise it. They make light of it. Whether they are around the table or not really does not matter to them. Some think the breaking of bread is such a small thing that they do not care whether they are present or not. Many of God's people abstain from the table, or just come once in a great while if they feel like it. If they do not feel like it, they do not come. That is making light of it.

Think of God who invites us to this table. Can we just despise it? If we really know what the breaking of bread is, can we abstain from it? You may be absent from other meetings but certainly not from this one. Of course, if possible, attend all meetings, but if you cannot, this is the one time that you must be present. The King has invited you to His own table for His Son, and how can we despise it? How sad it is today that we find God's people are so careless about breaking bread together. We need to see that this is the one time that everyone must be present, and not only present, but we must be prepared.

If you were invited to a dinner by the President of the United States, wouldn't you prepare yourself? Certainly you would. You would prepare yourself in every way, not only in the kind of clothing that would be proper for the occasion, but you would also try to know all the ways of etiquette for that particular time. Can we then come to the Lord's Table, being invited by the King of kings and the Lord of lords, and not be prepared?

This parable also has a humorous note to it. When those people who were invited refused to come, the master said, "Go out to the highways and byways and force people to come so that the house may be filled." And the house was filled, but when the master came in and noticed that one of those present did not have on the wedding garment, he said, "How camest thou in here not having on a wedding garment?" (Matthew 22:12). And he was cast out. The background for this was that in the early days, when a king, a nobleman, or a rich man invited guests to his table, he prepared the robes. Everyone who came in would put on the robe that he had prepared. You could not come with your own robe, but this man evidently thought his robe was good enough or even better, so he refused the robe which the host prepared for him. Because of that, he was cast out. Of course, there is an important truth involved in this concerning the kingdom, but we will not go into that. Concerning the Lord's Table, we need to be prepared beforehand.

Come in a Worthy Manner

We are coming to eat and drink of the Lord, and because of this, we have to come in a worthy manner; that is, in a manner that is worthy of the Lord. If there is any unconfessed sin in your life, if there is any controversy or disobedience to the Lord, if there is any unforgiving spirit towards your brother or sister, then this would be coming in an unworthy manner. Therefore, during the week in our homes, we must be before the Lord, asking Him to show us if there are any of these things. If there are, confess them, claim the blood of our Lord Jesus to be cleansed and purified, and thus we can come in a worthy manner. Otherwise, we will be eating our own sin, and this is a serious matter. So it is important that we are prepared before we come to the breaking of bread. If there is no opportunity for corporate preparation, then at least, privately, we need to prepare for it.

Bring Something to the Lord

Our preparation must not only be negative, but it must also be positive. It means that before we come to the Lord's Table, let us prepare to bring something to the Lord. We do not come to His Table empty-handed. Suppose someone has invited you into their home. Will you not bring something to show your appreciation—maybe some flowers or candy? Now the Lord invites you to His Table. Can we come empty-handed? Is it not right for us to bring something to Him to show our appreciation? Certainly, this is what we should do.

In the Old Testament time, the children of Israel never came to the temple empty-handed. They would always bring something with them. It would be something with which the Lord had blessed them, something they had worked hard for. They were in the promised land, and the blessing of the Lord was upon that land. The rain would fall in the right season, but they still had to work hard. So, by the combination of the blessing of God and their hard labor, they had produce. They would take what God had given them, the first-fruits, the best of everything, and bring it with them to the temple when they came to worship God.

… and they shall not appear before the LORD empty-handed. (Deuteronomy 16:16 NKJV).

If this was true with the children of Israel, physically, then it ought to be true with the church, spiritually, today. We have to come with our hands filled—filled with what the Lord has given us through the week in our reading the Word, in our prayer life, in His dealing with us and our dealing with Him, in our trials, in our triumphs, in all the circumstances of our lives. Whatever the Lord has enabled us to learn in all these things we bring it forth as produce; it may be a word, a song, or a revelation. We prepare it, put it in our basket, and bring it to the time of the breaking of bread. But oftentimes, we come empty-handed. We have not brought anything and, because of that, there is very little expression of our worship to Him.

Now this is a time that every brother and sister should bring something. It is not the time to come and receive anything. You come to bring something and lay it at the feet of our Lord Jesus, both the young and old. Do not think that because you are young you are not expected to bring anything. You are expected to bring something. This is the preparation that we need to have before we come to the Lord's Table.

Come with an Open Spirit

Now that we have come here and each one brings something let us lay it at the feet of our Lord and say, "Lord, this is something that I have brought to show my appreciation. I just put it at your feet. Use it as You see fit." In other words, because this is corporate worship, we must remember that at the Lord's Table, the Holy Spirit is present. The presence of the Lord himself is represented by the Holy Spirit. He is in charge of the feast. At the breaking of bread, you do not have certain brothers in charge of the time; the

Lord himself is the Host. The Holy Spirit is present, and He is in charge of this time and, because He is, everyone must come with an open spirit. Do not come with a closed spirit. That is to say, do not come and say, "I am not going to open my mouth," or "I must do something." We come with an open spirit, with an open heart saying, "Lord, we come here to worship You, and we expect Your Holy Spirit to guide and lead us in worship."

We do not know how to worship corporately, but the Holy Spirit is responsible for corporate worship. Therefore, every one of us must come with an open spirit. We must be so open to the Holy Spirit that whenever He wants to use any one of us, He can do so. Or when He thinks that this is not the time for us to speak, He can lead us to be silent. Sometimes, we cannot be quiet, and at other times, we cannot be used to speak. This is all self. It is not the Holy Spirit. We have to be so open that He can use us as He wishes.

There are two reasons for this. One is that when God's people are together, and everyone has their hands filled, there is such abundance that it will take eternity to have all of these expressions. Thank God for eternity! But we are still living in time. So when we do come together and bring what the Lord has given us, we have to let the Holy Spirit choose what pleases Him.

The second reason is that when the Holy Spirit is in charge, He is leading the body. It is not just the Holy Spirit leading individuals. There is the Holy Spirit's leading in our individual life, but when God's people come together to break bread, this leading of the Holy Spirit is corporate in nature.

Remember, He is leading the whole body, and as He is doing that, there is a symphony, a harmony. He will choose the things that we have brought with us, and He will order them in such a way that they will come forth as a beautiful symphony, all in harmony. There is no discord, no jarring note—whether it is praises, prayers, words, singing—everything is just as the Holy Spirit leads. As He comes upon this one and that one and takes up this and that, they will all come together as one great symphony. It will build up in worship until the peak is reached; then that is the time to break the bread.

So at the breaking of bread, there is a need not only for an open spirit but to exercise understanding and self-control. When the Holy Spirit leads, there is a divine order. When the wind blows, there is a direction. We will all follow in that direction, and then God will be pleased with our worship.

Reading to Break the Bread

When we come to break the bread, the center of our attraction is on the Table—the loaf and the cup. It is the Lord himself that we come to remember, to wor-ship, and to praise. This is not the time that we come to ask for something. It is the time that we come to give back to Him what He has given us. This is not the time that we think of ourselves; it is the time that we think of Him. Sometimes, when we come together, some will start to pray for this or that, asking for this and asking for that. Or sometimes, we just think of ourselves saying, "Oh, how unworthy I am, how sinful I am," instead of thinking more of the Lord. We should forget ourselves and concentrate on the Lord. Whether it is hymns, choruses, songs, praises, prayers or reading some word, let all be focused upon the Lord, and when the atmosphere or the spirit of worship ascends to a point, then we should start to break the bread and drink the cup.

In fact, the Scripture really does not specify or de-scribe to us how to conduct this meeting of the breaking of bread. The only thing we know that is prescribed is in I Corinthians 11: "The Lord took bread, and having given thanks broke it, and said, This is my body, which is for you: this do in remembrance of me. In like manner also the cup, after having supped, saying, This cup is the new covenant in my blood: this do, as often as ye shall drink it, in remembrance of me" (vv.23b-25). This is the only portion that is specified because it is up to the Holy Spirit. But there is one part that is prescribed—we break the bread, and we drink the cup.

In a sense, we need to learn not to drag on. The reason we drag on is that we come without preparation, so we have to spend lots of time just to prepare ourselves for the moment.

Secondly, it is because we do not understand how the Holy Spirit works in a meeting. If we are all prepared when we come together, maybe in five minutes, we are ready to break the bread. But if we are not prepared, it takes us more than half an hour to get there. It is a spiritual thing. If we are not there, we are not there; but if we are all prepared, we can just come together and, maybe in five minutes, it is time to break the bread. And if it is time to break the bread, break it.

Often, the prayer and the praise will come to a kind of peak, and people just wait; then it goes down again and picks up once more. It may do this two or three times, and by the time they break the bread, everyone is exhausted. Now do not do that. When the Spirit is there, let's break the bread. Some brother can either pray or start it. We break the bread at the time when our spirits are ready for it.

A Divine Order

There is another good practice that I will mention, not as a rule, but as a help. I do believe that there is a divine order at the breaking of bread. Before we break bread, all of our concentration is upon the Lord himself, remembering Him, being in communion with Him, thinking of Him and what He has done for us. But after we have broken bread, very often that is the end of the meeting because it has been an hour already. We have dragged so long that it is about time for the children to go, and we miss something. The breaking of bread should be the peak of the meeting, the climax, not the end. Our Lord Jesus, after He had broken bread, led His disciples to the Father. We not only have the record of His prayer in John 17 but after the supper it says they sang a song, and the Lord led them to Gethsemane. There our Lord presented himself before the Father. Psalm 22 has these words:

Save me from the lion's mouth. Yea, from the horns of the buffaloes hast thou answered me. I will declare thy name unto my brethren, in the midst of the congregation will I praise thee. (vv. 21-22)

In other words, after the bread is broken, we know that God is not only His God but our God, not only His Father but our Father. So He leads His own to the Father to worship Him who is the source of everything. The Lord said, "I will declare Your Name among my brethren and I will sing praises to Thee in the congregation." So there is a part that we can miss, not purposely, but because we do not understand too well. After we have broken bread, after we have experienced what the Lord has done for us, no doubt He will lead us back to the Father. If the breaking of bread is not prolonged, then we will have time to worship the Father, telling Him how much we appreciate Him.

For instance, this morning, at first, we were beholding the grace of our Lord Jesus, and that grace *is* our Lord Jesus. But after we experienced this grace by breaking bread, should we not see the love of God the Father? It is the love of God that gives us such grace, and should we not come to God our Father and thank Him for such love in giving Christ to us? That will lead us back to God, back to the Father, and bring us into that family relationship.

This is not a rule. It is not a law. And if we do not have the time to do it, then do not do it. Or if the Holy Spirit does not give us the burden to do it, just omit it. But it would be good if we had the understanding that at the breaking of bread we actually have these two parts: the before and the afterward. *Before* we partake of the bread and cup, our worship is centered upon the Lord Jesus. *After* we have remembered Him, our worship is centered upon the Father. We come to the Father through the Son. I believe that if the Lord should lead us in this way, then we will have a fuller worship experience.

5—Worship and Prayer

Matthew 6:9-13—Thus therefore pray ye: Our Father who art in the heavens, let thy name be sanctified, let thy kingdom come, let thy will be done as in heaven so upon the earth; give us to-day our needed bread, and forgive us our debts, as we also forgive our debtors, and lead us not into temptation, but save us from evil.

The Prayer Life of Our Lord Jesus

If you study the life of our Lord Jesus in the gospels, you will see that His life, even though He is the Son of God, was saturated throughout with prayers. I think it would be good if you could go through the gospels and make a study of every place where our Lord Jesus prayed. You would find how His life was saturated, permeated with prayers. His prayer was not only an indication of how utterly dependent He was upon His Father, but it was also an expression of His constant communion with the Father. Even though He was able to do things that ordinary people could not do, yet He said, "The Son can do nothing of himself save whatever he sees the Father doing" (John 5:19b). He never did anything without prayer. His prayer was His very life; it was the very breath of His life.

Prayer at His Baptism

Also, you will find that in His prayers there was always the spirit of worship. The first mention in the Bible of our Lord Jesus praying was when He was baptized. In Luke 3, we are told that after He was baptized and as He was praying, the Holy Spirit descended upon Him as a dove. The heavens were opened, and a voice said, "Thou art my beloved Son, in thee I have found my delight" (Luke 3:22b). Of course, He prayed before this, but this was the first mention in the Scripture, and it was in connection with His baptism.

What is baptism to Him? When the Lord came to John the Baptist to be baptized, John forbade Him. He would not do it for Him because He sensed that there was no need for Him to be baptized. The baptism of John was the baptism of repentance, and yet Jesus had nothing to repent. But our Lord Jesus said, "Let's do it for righteousness' sake" (see Matthew 3:15). In other words, when our Lord Jesus came to be baptized of John, it was not because He needed it; it was because at that moment He offered himself as a sacrifice for our sins. He was willing to take our place of repentance. He was willing to go into the water, into death that He might save us. In His baptism, He was offering himself voluntarily; no one forced Him to do it. There was no reason that He should do it. He was not obligated in any sense, yet He voluntarily and willingly gave himself to God as a sacrifice for our sins.

When He came out of the water, the Bible says He was praying. Now the Bible does not tell us what He was praying, but I do believe if we consider the situation, He certainly was not asking God for something. Very often, we think of prayer as asking or petition. We want something, so we pray and ask God to give it to us. But when our Lord Jesus stepped out of the water and was praying, surely He was not asking for something for himself. At this time, when He was praying, after He had just offered himself as a sacrifice to God, certainly He was worshiping God. His very baptism was worship—giving himself to God the Father that He might use Him as He willed so that God's purpose might be fulfilled. It was praying that His offering might be accepted and would please the Father. It was completely selfless, and we know worship is a selfless adoration that goes out to God. That is worship.

So I do believe, even though the Bible does not record His prayer and only tells that He was praying, we can understand that it was not petition as such, but it must have been a going-out of His whole being to God in adoration, in love, offering himself as a sacrifice. And because of this, the Holy Spirit came upon Him and abode upon Him like a dove. Do you know what the dove represents? Why is it that on the day of Pentecost, the Holy Spirit came down on the people as tongues of fire, and here in this instance, the Holy Spirit came upon the Lord as a dove? A dove is the sacrifice of the poor. A poor person cannot offer a bullock, nor even a sheep or a lamb. A poor person is allowed to offer a dove or a pigeon, and here our Lord Jesus offered himself as a sacrifice for the poor. The Holy Spirit came upon Him as a dove and dwelt in Him because it is by the eternal Spirit that He offered himself unto God. The heavens were opened, and a voice said, "This is my beloved Son in whom I have found my delight" (Matthew 3:17b). In other words, the Father was pleased with what He did. The Father was really worshiped through His action and His prayer. So, let's remember that worship and prayer cannot be separated. Unless we pray with a worshiping spirit, it is no prayer at all.

Five Factors of Prayer

The word *prayer* is such a comprehensive term. Someone has said that prayer can include these five factors.

Adoration—Prayer is adoration, and adoration is the soul lost in wonder, in the worship of God. When you approach God, when the sense of God is so real, then you are lost in wonder and amazement that He is such a God and can do such things. It is almost speechless, yet it is prayer. Prayer is the soul lost in wonder, lost in the worship of God.

Thanksgiving—Prayer is thanksgiving. It is the heart overflowing in gratitude for His abundant mercies. Why do we give thanks? Because we are simply overwhelmed by what He has done for us by His many mercies. That is the reason we give Him thanks. Thanksgiving is prayer.

Confession—Prayer is confession. It is the expression in words of genuine contrition in the sense that we have failed God, that we have not attained to divine standards. As we confess our shortcomings, our failures, and our sins before God, it is prayer. Confession is prayer.

Petition—Prayer is petition. It is the laying before God of our personal needs, and probably, to most people, this is prayer. We have personal needs, and we lay them before God and ask our heavenly Father to supply these needs. Certainly, this is prayer. It is petition.

Intercession—Prayer is intercession. Not only do we pray for ourselves, asking for our own needs, but we make requests for other people—people who are not so privileged as we are, who may not have such ready access to the throne of grace. Therefore, we take it upon ourselves to intercede for other people.

A well-balanced devotional life, a prayer life, should be composed of these five elements: petition for ourselves, intercessions for others, confession of our shortcomings, thanksgiving for all that He has done for us, and adoration for who He is. These five elements compose what the Scripture calls prayer. Of course, the first element, adoration, is the most basic.

So in this first mention of the prayer of our Lord Jesus, you can see the spirit of adoration in Him—how His whole being just went out to God, considering God as worthy to have everything.

Prayer and Fasting

The next mention of our Lord praying is in Matthew 4:1. After He was baptized, He was led by the Spirit into the wilderness to be tempted by the enemy. The Bible says He fasted forty days and forty nights. Even though the word *prayer* is not used here, no doubt, during those forty days and forty nights when He was fasting, He was praying because fasting is not something that you do for the sake of fasting. You fast in order to pray. Therefore, you cannot separate fasting and praying. When you fast, you deny yourself. As it is said in the Old Testament, you afflict your soul. Fasting is to weaken the soul's power so that you may concentrate on prayer in the power of the Spirit.

In the world, other than Christianity, people practice fasting. Fasting is not something that only Christians do. In other religions of the world, you do find fasting. But the fasting that the world practices is very different from the fasting that is practiced by Christians. The fasting that the world practices is to release soul power—not to weaken it but to strengthen it. However, fasting with Christians is to weaken the soul power and to release the power of the Spirit. So there is a vast difference between fasting in the world and fasting with Christians.

Why do we fast? Why do we afflict our souls? Why do we lay down our legitimate requirements of life? It is for the purpose of prayer. It is not in any sense that we, by afflicting our souls and using this self-affliction, hope to touch the heart of God. No! That is not the meaning of fasting. Fasting is that we are so intense before God, seeking His will and desiring to do it, that we are willing to deny ourselves and lay ourselves aside so that we may not in any way interfere with God.

So here we see our Lord Jesus in the wilderness fasting forty days and forty nights. As He was fasting, He was afflicting His soul; He was laying himself down completely. There was not a trace of self in Him through fasting and praying. That is why, when the enemy came to tempt Him afterward, He could give these answers. In every instance there was none of self but all of God:

Man shall not live by bread alone, but by every word which goes out through God's mouth (Matthew 4:4).

Thou shalt not tempt the Lord thy God (4:7).

Thou shalt do homage to the Lord thy God, and him alone shalt thou serve (4:10).

Now that is prayer. Prayer is the laying down of one's self and letting God, at His will, be everything.

Very often when we pray, we want God to do what we wish. In other words, if our prayers are answered, it would just increase our ego. When we pray, do we lay ourselves down completely, wanting nothing but himself and His will, wanting Him to be exalted and ourselves to be humbled? If that kind of spirit is in us, that is praying. We can never separate worship from prayer. It is in a worshiping spirit that we enter into prayer, and the result of prayer is worship. After we have prayed, our prayer is answered, and we find ourselves in worship to God.

Prayer Early in the Morning

Another instance is found in Mark 1. Early in the morning before the day broke, our Lord Jesus went out to the wilderness to pray. When the day dawned, many people would flock to Him. There would be many things to do. He would be occupied every hour, almost every minute, and knowing this, He rose up before the day broke. He went there early to pray. Again, we do not know what He was praying because it is not recorded in the Bible. But the Lord being the Son of David, I think we can use David's words to give us a clue as to what our Lord Jesus must have been praying early in the morning. For example, look at Psalm 5, and we often say this Psalm is a morning hymn.

Jehovah, in the morning shalt thou hear my voice; in the morning will I address myself to thee, and will look up. For thou art not a God that hath pleasure in wickedness; evil shall not sojourn with thee (5:3-4).

Again in Psalm 57, *Of David*:

Awake, my glory; awake, lute and harp: I will wake the dawn. I will give thee thanks among the peoples, O Lord; of thee will I sing psalms among the nations: For thy lovingkindness is great unto the heavens, and thy truth unto the clouds (vv. 8-10).

Then in Psalm 63, a Psalm of David, we read:

O God, thou art my God; early will I seek thee. My soul thirsteth for thee, my flesh languisheth for thee in a dry and weary land without water (v. 1).

Through the mouth of David we can see what the Son of David, who is also the Lord of David, would pray in the early morning. He would certainly be seeking the face of His Father—"early will I seek Thee." How He longed for God. His soul languished for God. He was there seeking God, declaring what a God He was—His lovingkindness, His justice, His tender mercies, His truth. So the early morning prayer of our Lord Jesus was certainly the seeking of His Father's face—to behold Him, to gaze upon Him in adoration, in love, and in thanksgiving and praise. There is no doubt that would be the main part of His morning prayer.

It really is a good practice to rise early in the morning because after the day breaks and all the many things of life begin to crowd upon you, you will find it very difficult to be set apart to commune with God, to seek His face, to behold Him, and to worship Him. It is good that we start our day with Him, that before we do anything or see any face, we would see the face of God. As the Psalmist says, "I will wake the dawn"; it is not just early rising, but to rise that you may have a time with God. Our Lord Jesus, throughout His entire earthly life, had that life with God as indicated in His early morning prayer. How much we need this! How much we need to just draw near to God in the silence of the morning and there behold Him, to give Him thanks and praise!

Prayer through the Night

Another instance we will look at is in Luke 6: "And it came to pass in those days that he went out into the mountain to pray, and he spent the night in prayer to God" (verse 12). He not only prayed early in the morning but He prayed through the night. We do not know what He was praying since it was not recorded, but we can see what He must have prayed about because He chose the twelve to be His disciples the next morning. So no doubt through the night He was praying, seeking the Father's will concerning those whom He should choose as His disciples, those who were to be with Him, trained and sent by Him. Now this is not a small thing. If we knew those twelve whom He chose or if we know ourselves, probably we would wonder if He would ever choose us. No doubt, our Lord Jesus knew these twelve men so well, and so far as His humanity was concerned, He knew choosing the twelve would be such a trial to Him—every one of them. Humanly speaking, He would have been much happier by staying alone. What patience He must have exercised to be with these twelve, day and night, training them to be sent out as His representatives. Humanly speaking, our Lord Jesus would never have chosen them. Never! But He was praying through the night, laying down himself, giving up His life, seeking the Father's will, and it was only then and there that He was able to come down from the mountain and choose those twelve precious men, especially Judas Iscariot. He knew that this man would betray Him, but He chose him to be with Him and watch Him day and night. This is prayer.

Our Lord Jesus was praying and, in praying, He was giving up His will and was taking the Father's will even if it meant trials, tribulations, and thorns. Paul had only one thorn, but our Lord had twelve thorns in His body. These were thorns to Him, yet He chose them because it was the Father's will, and that was done through prayer.

Do we pray like this? When we pray, are we trying to twist the arm of God to do our will? Or when we pray, are we allowing Him to put us to death that His will may be done even if it means a hardship, maybe a thorn to us? Are we willing to accept it? That is prayer, and that is what you will find our Lord Jesus was praying. Of course, you can go through the gospels and find many, many more instances, and all of them will indicate to us what prayer really is. Prayer is worship because it is exalting God. It is giving God His place. It is the laying down of ourselves; it is glorifying God. It is for God's will and purpose to be done. Also, prayer has to be prayed in the spirit of worship.

In Matthew 6:9 and Luke 11:1, our Lord Jesus was praying, and one of the disciples came to Him and said, "Lord, teach us to pray." Our Lord answered, "When you pray, say Our Father." Often, we say this is the Lord's prayer, but actually, it is the prayer of the church. The Lord is teaching His church to pray, so the Lord's prayer actually is the prayer of the church.

Corporate Prayer

Before we go into this incident that is recorded, I would like to use this opportunity to say something about corporate prayer. The so-called Lord's prayer is a corporate prayer. It is the prayer of the church. This is why it begins with, "*Our* Father," not "*My* Father." So far as the nature of prayer is concerned, there is no difference between private or personal prayer and public or corporate prayer. In other words, you do not pray in one spirit when you are praying alone and in another spirit when you are praying with your brothers and sisters. The spiritual nature of prayer is the same whether praying alone or with your brothers and sisters. You do not have to put on something extra when praying with your brothers and sisters.

In nature, prayer is always the same. But there is a difference in the *way* or practice of prayer. In corporate prayer, there is an added dimension. Now it is not only between you and the Lord, but there are brothers and sisters with you. In corporate prayer you have an added dimension, a horizontal relationship, whereas in private prayer you only have a vertical relationship. This difference affects the way we pray and also the subject or content of our prayer.

You are Not Alone

First of all, you will find that it says, "Our Father, who art in heaven." *Our* Father. Now, what do you mean by this word *our*? *Our* shows you that you are not alone. It is not *I*, *me*, *my*. It is *our*. It means that when you pray, you do not pray as one person, but you pray as representing a group of people—"Our Father." You cannot say *our* if you are not part of a group. The word *our* means we share the same Father; we are one. He is our Father, and as we pray, we pray with one accord. You cannot just pray your own prayer because when you come to pray, you pray the prayer of the church. When you are praying, you are representing all the brothers and sisters. You are not just offering your personal prayer. Or to put it in another way, when you pray, you include your brothers and sisters in your prayer. Many but one—one yet many. Now this is the corporateness in prayer. So when we come together to pray, remember that each time you pray you do not pray as on your own. You are representing the brothers and sisters there. You are just a mouthpiece of the church, and you voice the burden that is upon the church. Also, if we pray as one man, with our prayers representing the whole church, you will find there is tremendous power that you do not find in a personal, individual prayer.

No Need for Vain Repetition

Another point to remember when we are praying together as one man is that there is no need for vain repetition. This does not mean that you do not repeat because even our Lord Jesus repeated in His prayers. In the garden of Gethsemane, He prayed three times, repeating himself. In II Corinthians, Paul also repeated himself three times. So it does not mean that we cannot repeat. If repetition is for emphasis, you can do it because it is not vain repetition.

What is the difference? Suppose in a prayer meeting the burden is to pray for the conference, and you feel burdened to pray for the ministry. So you begin to ask the Lord to give the word to those who will minister and, as you pray, you represent the whole company that is present. You are not just praying on your own. You are praying with all your brothers and sisters. But after you finish praying for the ministry, probably another brother or sister is still burdened with it. In other words, the burden has not been discharged fully, and another brother or sister will take it up and ask the Lord to really bless the ministry that it might speak out God's heart and mind for that moment. Now, this is not vain repetition; this is emphasis.

What is vain repetition? It is going through the motions without really meaning it. For instance, when we are together praying as one man, often we will say, "Lord, we come to You and claim the blood of our Lord Jesus that the throne of grace may be opened to us." After one brother prays this, another brother will say the same thing, and then the third will do likewise—not in any sense of emphasis but in the sense of habit. There is no need for it because we pray as one man, and what our brother has already prayed, we pray with him. So it has been prayed, and you do not need to repeat it. There is no need for it unless you feel it deeply. Now that is different.

Let Your Prayer Be to the Point

In corporate prayer, we pray as one man. In order that we may do it well, our prayers should be shorter. In personal prayer, you may spend an hour praying and going through all kinds of things that are upon your heart, but in corporate prayer, do not take up too many things because you are not alone. Let your brothers and sisters have a chance to pray. But on the other hand, do not give all the chance to your brothers and sisters. Let your prayer be short—to the point. Do not take up too many things—maybe one aspect of one thing. That is enough.

Let All Pray

Also, in corporate prayer, it is important that we all pray. Everyone is a priest, and everyone should learn to pray. Everyone should learn to be an expression for the whole body. Do not allow the enemy to shut your mouth. This is our privilege. So in a prayer time, we do urge all the brothers and sisters to pray. It is not for a few to pray all the time, and the others never open their mouths. We must all be open to the Lord and learn to take the burden and be the vessel or instrument in God's hand to utter it for the whole company. This is our privilege.

Learn to Take Up Burden

There is another thing concerning corporate prayer, and that is you have to learn to take the burden. In personal prayer, it is easier because you just pray what you are burdened with. But when you come to a prayer time, and things are mentioned for prayer, you may not be burdened with them. Either you do not know about them beforehand, or even after they are mentioned, you do not think it has anything to do with you. Very often, we are overburdened with our own burdens, and we cannot take up any more. So when we come to a time of corporate prayer, let's leave all of our personal burdens behind and come with open hearts, ready to receive whatever burden the Lord may give to His church for that moment. We need to learn to take the burden. You may not be burdened with it, but if you are open to it and if the Spirit of the Lord gives that burden to the church, then since you are a member of the body of Christ, you will certainly be burdened by it. Because of this, you will be able to discharge it in prayer.

When something very personal is the topic of prayer—maybe a brother or sister is sick or in trouble—it seems to be always true that we can take up that burden very quickly. But when we come to bigger things, it seems that they are too big for us to take up, and they become vague and general. It becomes difficult for us to take them up. We need to learn to have our hearts enlarged that we may be able to take up more burdens, not just small things but also bigger things that we may really be a house of prayer for all nations—and this is what we are.

So I have just mentioned a few things to show that in corporate prayer, there is much that we need to learn in order to fulfill our function. Prayer is the ministry of the church. It is the corporate expression of our continuing in the teaching and the fellowship of the apostles.

The Prayer of the Church

Now we come to the so-called Lord's prayer. It is actually the prayer of the church. How does the Lord Jesus teach us to pray? Now everybody knows the Lord is not teaching us to repeat these words. You can repeat it if your spirit is there, but what the Lord is giving us is the principle, and you will find it begins with worship.

Our Father which art in heaven, Hallowed be thy name. Thy kingdom come, Thy will be done in earth, as it is in heaven (Matthew 6:9b-10 KJV).

That is worship.

Our Father, who art in heaven.

When you mention that, it is as if we turn our eyes upon our Father who art in heaven. We look at Him with wonder and adoration.

Hallowed be Thy name.

We exalt Him. We see His worth. We declare His worthiness. That is worship.

Thy kingdom come.
Thy will be done
on earth as it is in heaven.

In other words, it is for the Lord's will to be done that we pray for His kingdom to come. Now that is worship.

So in corporate prayer, it begins with worship, and, in that worshiping spirit, we are led into petition and intercession and confession.

Give us this day our daily bread.

That is for the physical needs of God's people.

Forgive us our debts as we forgive our debtors.

This is for the soulical needs of God's people. In our soul there must be peace and rest, and if we have an unforgiving spirit—something we will not forgive—it affects our soul.

Lead us not into temptation
but deliver us from the evil one.

This is for our spiritual needs. Our physical needs, our psychological needs, and our spiritual needs are all being brought to God as our petition and our intercession—not only for ourselves but for the whole church, for all God's people.

Then in some manuscripts it says,

For thine is the kingdom, and the power, and the glory, for ever. Amen (Matthew 6:13b KJV).

Again it ends with worship. So let us remember that you really cannot separate prayer from worship. A person who is not in a worshiping spirit cannot pray. And the prayer that is answered is prayed in a spirit of worship.

Given to Prayer

In the early church, even before the day of Pentecost, the 120 who had gathered together, gave themselves to continual prayer with one accord (see Acts 1:14). That is how the church began. Those people gave themselves to prayer; they were not just passively waiting for the power from on high. They gave them-selves actively to prayer and, as they were praying, they were guided by the Holy Spirit to fill up any gap that might be in their midst. In other words, through prayer, they were ready; they were prepared for the outpouring of the Holy Spirit.

Pray with One Accord

In Acts 4, when Peter and John returned and reported to the church the council's persecution, they prayed with one voice. Now I often wonder how you can pray with one voice. How can you pray with one accord? How can you agree in prayer? That seems to be the most difficult thing in corporate prayer. In personal prayer, you just need to agree with yourself, but in corporate prayer you have to agree with your brothers and sisters. And this is not agreement by negotiation or by compromise. Certainly not. But the problem is how can we come to one voice, one mind, one thought, agreement with one accord? Notice that when they prayed together, they lifted up their voice and said, "Lord, thou art the God who made the heaven and the earth and the sea, and all that is in them" (Acts 4:24). It is worship. "And now, Lord, look upon their threatenings, and give to thy bondmen with all boldness to speak thy word" (Acts 4:29). In other words, when these people came together to pray, they were all fully committed to God and His testimony. No one said, "Lord, persecution is coming. Help us to escape it. Do not allow it to get worse." No! No one was praying for himself. Everyone was concerned with God's testimony and they were people who were fully committed to God's testimony—no matter what happened to them. They were not thinking of themselves; they were only thinking of what would happen to the testimony of God.

They asked God to give them boldness—not to retreat but to advance. That is the reason they could pray with one voice. Very often, when we cannot pray with one voice, it is because we are not fully committed. *Dear brothers and sisters, praying is not playing*. If we are not fully committed to God and to His testimony, there is no use to pray. And we cannot pray with one accord because everyone has his own thought. But when we come together as a committed people to God and to His testimony, then I do believe it is an easy thing for us to pray with one accord because we all agree with Him. We do not need to ask people to agree with us, nor for us to agree with people. We all agree with Him, and as we agree with Him, we can pray with one voice as we are moved by the Spirit of God.

Remember this: They could pray together because they had a worshiping spirit, and, with such a spirit of worship, they could pray as one man. So, may the Lord help us.

6—Worship and Work

Matthew 4: 10b—Thou shalt do homage [worship] to the Lord thy God, and him alone shalt thou serve.

John 6:28-29—They said therefore to him, What should we do that we may work the works of God? Jesus answered and said to them, This is the work of God, that ye believe on him whom he has sent.

Ephesians 2:10—For we are his workmanship, having been created in Christ Jesus for good works, which God has before prepared that we should walk in them.

Ezekiel 44:15-16—But the priests, the Levites, the sons of Zadok, that kept the charge of my sanctuary when the children of Israel went astray from me, they shall approach unto me to minister unto me, and they shall stand before me to present unto me the fat and the blood, saith the Lord Jehovah. They shall enter into my sanctuary, and they shall approach unto my table, to minister unto me, and they shall keep my charge.

We are still considering this matter of worship. What is worship? Therefore, this time we would like to enter into the area of worship and work. First of all, we need to define what work is; that is, work according to the Scripture. What is God's work? Many may work for God, but they may not be working God's work.

You remember how that great Pharisee Saul persecuted the followers of the Lord Jesus. He thought he was working for God. He thought he was doing God's work, and he certainly was very diligent in doing it. He did not know that he was doing the very opposite, that he was against the work of God instead of doing God's work. Later on, the Lord met him on the road to Damascus, and he was converted. Then he really served the Lord in spirit and with a conscience void of offense. Yet still, the Jews considered him as working against God. So you see this whole matter of work is really a problem.

What is God's work? What does it mean to do God's work? How do we know if we are doing God's work? Are we just working for God as we think we ought to?

One day, we shall all appear at the judgment seat of Christ. And when we do, we will get the surprise of our life because many people will come to Him and say, "Lord, did we not perform miracles and wonders in Thy name? Did we not cast out demons in Thy name? Did we not even preach in Thy name?" And the Lord said, "I do not know you. Depart from me, workers of lawlessness" (see Matthew 7:22-23). Well, they did work, and they even worked in the name of the Lord; yet the Lord said, "You are workers of lawlessness. You are not doing My work. You may be working for me as you think, but I do not know you."

How do we know that we are doing God's work? Are we just working for God in our own way? To do God's work is to do His will. To do God's will is to do it in the power of the Holy Spirit. In order to do God's work, there is a prerequisite, and that is we must first believe in Him. You remember the story recorded in John 6 how our Lord Jesus fed five thousand with two loaves and five fishes. The next day the crowd sought after Him, and He said to them, "Work not for the food which perishes, but for the food which abides unto life eternal" (John 6:27). So the Jews said, "What should we do that we may work the works of God? Jesus answered and said to them, This is the work of God, that ye believe on him whom he has sent" (John 6:28b-29).

When the Lord mentioned this whole matter of work, the Jews said, "Now, what should we do? What do we do that we may do the works of God?" In other words, their whole concept about work was: "Let's do something. Let's do something for God, and then we will be doing the works of God." But the answer of our Lord surprised them because He said, "This is the work of God, that ye believe on him whom he has sent." They wanted to do something, but the Lord said, "No, believe in what God has already done for you."

What is God's work? Basically, it is not something that you do; it is something that you believe. He has done it, and you just believe in what He has done. Therefore, the work of God is based on faith. Without faith, you cannot do God's work.

"How much rather shall the blood of the Christ, who by the eternal Spirit offered himself spotless to God, purify your conscience from dead works to worship the living God?" (Hebrews 9:14). We think that if we work for God, if we do something, if we accumulate merits, then we are worshiping God. But the Lord said that we need the blood to purify our conscience from dead works to worship the living God. Now there is a connection between worship and work. Ordinarily, people think that if they do something good, if they accumulate some merits, if they do some good things for God, then surely they are worshiping God. But remember, this is just bribing their conscience; it is dead work. Work without faith is dead work. It is just like the offering of Cain. He took the best of the produce of the land and offered it, but there was no blood, there was no faith. It was just self-confidence.

He brought the best of his produce and offered it to God as worship—his own work as worship, his own merit as a worship. But he was rejected because his offering was rejected. He offered dead works to God. You cannot worship the living God with dead works.

First of all, your conscience needs to be purified by the blood from dead works. In other words, you have to recognize that every good work that you do, every merit that you accumulate, every righteousness that you think you have, without Christ, without faith, is all dead work. God cannot accept it. God cannot be worshiped by these dead works. Your conscience is being deceived into thinking that by bringing these merits and good works to God then certainly God is worshiped. Not at all! Not only will your worship be rejected, but as in the case of Cain, something terrible will happen.

Work Begins with Faith

First, you believe in what God has done for you in Christ, the One whom God has sent, in His finished work. It is done. Everything is done for you, and as you believe, you begin the doing of God's work. Also, as you believe, God's work will begin to work out through you. This is the work of God: believe in Him whom God has sent.

In Ephesians 2:10, we read, "For we are his work-manship, having been created in Christ Jesus for good works, which God has before prepared that we should walk in them." I think we are very familiar with Ephesians 2:8: "For ye are saved by grace, through faith." That is the foundation of our salvation. We are saved by grace through faith. But very often, we forget verse 10: "We are his workmanship." Before we can think of doing God's work, we must first see that we are God's workmanship; we are His work. We are God's workmanship created in Christ Jesus for good works—those good works that God has prepared beforehand for us to walk therein. God first works in us so that we may do His work, His will.

Work out your own salvation with fear and trembling, for it is God who works in you both the willing and the working according to his good pleasure (Philippians 2:12b-13).

When it comes to this matter of work, first of all, let us see that it has to begin with faith. We believe in His work, and as we do this and let Him work in us, then it will be worked out. And as it is worked out, we are doing God's work. Doing God's work is not just that we are doing something for Him. Doing God's work is that He himself is working in and through us. Are we doing God's work, or are we working for God?

Our Lord Jesus As the Worker

Look at our Lord Jesus. Certainly He is the Servant of the Lord; certainly He is the Worker. Now look at how He worked. In John 5 He said, "My Father worketh hitherto and I work. The Son can do nothing of himself save whatever he sees the Father doing: for whatever things he does, these things also the Son does in like manner" (vv.17,19). Our Lord Jesus healed a man who was infirm for thirty-eight years, but He healed him on the sabbath. So of course, He was accused of violating the sabbath. Yet our Lord Jesus answered and said, "My Father worketh unto now and I work. I can do nothing of Myself. I do it because I see My Father has done it. I am just doing what My Father has done or is doing. It is My Father who has done it in Me."

After our Lord Jesus had delivered the woman who had committed adultery, He said, "I do nothing of myself, but as the Father has taught me I speak these things" (John 8:28b). So the Lord Jesus said, "I can do nothing" (John 5); and then He said, "I do nothing" (John 8). In other words, with Him, it is the Father; it is not the work.

As you read the gospel according to John, you will find a word or phrase that is repeated again and again by the Lord: "My hour," or "My hour has not yet come."

In John 2, at the marriage of Cana, the mother of Jesus came to Him and said, "They have no wine" (John 2:3b). She was suggesting that her illustrious Son should do something to rescue the situation. But the Lord said, "Woman, (Now that is not a hard word. In Greek it means 'little woman,' and it is an affectionate word.) what have I to do with thee? My hour is not yet come."

In John 7, it says that one day the Lord's brothers, according to the flesh, said to Him, "Now if a person wants to get famous, he does not hide in the hills. Go to Jerusalem at the time of the feast and show yourself to them." The Lord replied, "Your time is always ready, but mine is not yet come." He always waited for that hour.

In John 12, some Greeks came to Andrew and Phillip and said, "We would like to see Jesus. So they reported it to our Lord and the Lord said, "My hour has now come. Glorify Thy Son that Thy Son may glorify Thee. Father, deliver me from this hour, but for this hour have I come."

In John 13, we see that our Lord knows His hour of departure has come, and He loved His own, and He loved them to the uttermost.

In John 17, He said, "This is the hour. Glorify Thy Son that Thy Son may glorify Thee."

Throughout our Lord's life, in His work, He was always waiting for the hour. He would never do anything before the hour came. What does it mean? It simply means He waited for the Father's will and the Father's time. He could do nothing by himself. To Him, the work is secondary; the Father is primary.

Or we may put it another way: work to Him is worship. It is not just doing something and finishing it. It is a form of worship. It is His way to express His worship to the Father—how He honored the Father, how He waited upon the Father, how He did the work and the will of the Father, how He glorified the Father. To the Lord Jesus, *that* is work. It is not just doing something. Even before He went to the cross, it was not the cross that He desired; it was the Father's will. "Not my will but Your will be done." It is the will of the Father that He should go to the cross, that He should drink the cup—and He will drink it. He will do it in spite of the tremendous cost that He has to pay because work to Him is a form of worship. He worshiped the Father with His work. He sought the Father's will, and He waited for the Father's time before He did anything. No wonder that all the works He did abound to the glory of the Father.

Work Does Not Replace Worship

On the other hand, our Lord was not slothful in any way about doing God's work. We see a perfect balance in the life of our Lord Jesus. On the one hand, He would do nothing before the time. He was never in a hurry. People tried to tempt Him, to hasten Him, but they could not. He would not be pushed. He was waiting before the Father, ministering to the Father (if we may say this) before He would minister to the people.

Yet, on the other hand, He was not in any way slothful. Even when He was twelve years old and He was made a Son of the Law, He tarried in Jerusalem as His parents began their journey back home. On the third day, His parents found Him in the temple, and there He was asking and answering questions. Mary said, "Son, why did You do this to us?" And our Lord Jesus said, "Why do you come and find me? Must I not be occupied with My Father's business?"

Even when He was twelve, He was engaged in the Father's business. He was doing God's work. But notice the Bible says that He went down with His parents and obeyed them. Suppose this had happened to you. What would you do? Would you say, "Must I not be occupied with my Father's business? Go home. I will stay here and work." Would this be the right thing to do?

We worship our work; we are not worshiping God. We may be so occupied with working for God that we have no time to worship God. In other words, worship and work become two separate things. Isn't it true that many servants of the Lord are so busy working for God that they have no time to pray? They have no time to wait upon the Lord. The more they work, the less they worship, and the result is that they worship their work.

But if work is really of God, you will find the more you work, the more you worship. The more you worship, the more you work because worship and work cannot be separated. Work comes out of worship. Work must be done in a worshiping spirit, and work will lead to worship. If it does not, then what is the work? Is it worthwhile? Will God receive anything?

Work Does Not Replace Doing the Father's Will

Even when our Lord Jesus was twelve years old and was so occupied with the Father's business, yet He went down with His parents and obeyed them because work was not the most important thing in His life. The Father's will was the most important thing. It was God's will that He should submit to His earthly parents until the time when God would manifest Him to the nation.

Our Lord was most earnest in God's work. In John 4, the Lord told His disciples,

Do not ye say, that there are yet four months and the harvest comes? Behold, I say to you, Lift up your eyes and behold the fields, for they are already white to harvest (v. 35).

Now that is work. Again, in chapter 11 our Lord Jesus said,

Are there not twelve hours in the day? If any one walk in the day, he does not stumble, because he sees the light of this world; but if any one walk in the night, he stumbles, because the light is not in him (vv. 9-10).

When it is night, no man can work. We have to work.

On the one hand, our Lord Jesus was very earnest, very diligent in doing God's work. He was never lazy; He never shrank back. Never! But on the other hand, work was not just meeting a need. Work is doing the Father's will. How often our work is determined by need. Yes, there is need everywhere, and because of these needs, we have to meet them; we have to work. It does not mean that we should neglect them, acting as though we have not seen these needs. Of course not! But what governs our work? Is it need or the Father's will? It was not need with our Lord Jesus; it was the Father's will because to Him, work is worship. He worshiped the Father by doing these works. They were never separated.

We Are All Workers

Dear brothers and sisters, how about us? In one sense, we are all workers. Sometimes it disturbs people when we say that only a few who are chosen work and the rest do not work or are not workers. Then who are the workers? Is it those who are especially called to preach? Are they the workers doing God's work? So what do we do? Do we just do our work? No.

But when we say that we are all workers, it also disturbs people, as if they do not want to work for God. Whether we are called to preach, to cook, to serve the table, or to minister the word, we are all workers in God's vineyard.

You remember that parable our Lord Jesus spoke in Matthew 20. A man had a vineyard and went out to engage workers in the early morning. They agreed on a certain wage—a denarius for a day's work. So these people went in and worked. Afterward, he went out and saw people standing idle and he engaged them also. Even at the last hour, just an hour before the work was finished, there were people still standing there idle, and the man said, "Why do you stand here all the day idle?" And they said, "No man has hired us." So the man said, "Come into my vineyard and work." Now what does it mean? It means that even at this late hour, we are all called into His vineyard—every one of us, every brother and sister. Do not think that you are not a worker. You are indeed God's worker. We are all called into God's vineyard to work in the field to produce fruit for His glory.

Or we may use another figure of speech: we are all laborers building on the foundation which is already laid, which is Christ Jesus. In I Corinthians 3, Paul said he was like a wise architect who has laid the foundation. And there cannot be any foundation other than Christ Jesus, and everyone is to build upon it. Every one of us is a builder, a worker. We are all working in God's vineyard, and God has only one vineyard. There is only one work. God's work is one and we are all engaged in doing that one work. God has only one building. He does not have a summer house and a winter house. He has only one building, and we are all building that building—the house of God. Everyone is employed. There is no unemployment in the kingdom of God. It is one hundred percent employment. Therefore, we cannot stand there idle; we have to work.

Work Comes out of Worship

Are we just working for God or are we doing God's work? Think of Martha and Mary. Our Lord Jesus came to the village, and Martha certainly wanted to entertain our Lord the best that she could. She was so busy cooking the best dishes and trying to do everything just right for the Lord. And she did it all with good intentions. She was serving the Lord and working for the Lord, but while she was doing that, she lost her worshiping spirit. She was disturbed by the many works that she had to do—setting the table, arranging the chairs, preparing the food, rushing in and out of the dining room and kitchen. Finally, she could not contain herself seeing her sister sitting at the feet of the Lord, quietly listening to Him. She just could not stand it anymore. But she was too polite to just call out to her to come and help since the Lord was there. So she did it in a nice way by saying, "Lord, don't you care? I am so busy, and my sister is just sitting there. Won't you tell her to come and help me?" And the Lord said, "Martha, Martha, you are busy with many works, but your sister has chosen the better portion" (see Luke 10:38-42).

What do you see here? You see Martha working for the Lord—so busy, but while she was working for the Lord, she lost her worship. Now Mary was sitting at the feet of the Lord listening. That is a position of worship. Because she listened to the Lord, does it mean that she will just sit there forever? No. One day, when the Lord was again being entertained, Mary came in with an alabaster flask of ointment. She broke it and anointed the Lord. How did she know the Lord was going to die? Even the disciples did not know it. The Lord told them at least three times, but they could not understand it. Why? And why was it that only Mary understood? She knew the Lord was going to die; therefore, she anointed Him to prepare for His burial. Where did she get the knowledge? It was while she was sitting at the feet of the Lord. Her work was anointing the Lord and the fragrance filled the house. Who served the Lord more, Martha or Mary? If work is just a work, God is not worshiped, but if work comes out of worship, it will be worship unto the Lord.

Ministering to the Lord

In Acts 13:2, in the church at Antioch, there were five prophets and teachers. The Bible says, "And as they were ministering to the Lord and fasting, the Holy Spirit said, Separate me now Barnabas and Saul for the work to which I have called them." These prophets and teachers were the people who ministered to the needs of the church. In the church at Antioch, there were many believers, and they needed to be fed, to be nourished by the word of God. These five prophets and teachers were raised up by God to minister to the needs of God's people there. But before they ministered to the people, they first ministered to the Lord, and out of their ministry to the Lord came forth that apostolic work.

When we are working, do we first minister to the Lord? Is our work the outcome of our ministering unto the Lord, or is it because we see some need and we do it?

This reminds us of Ezekiel 44. Ezekiel saw in a vision the house of God, the temple of God being restored and not only the house restored but the priestly ministry also. But notice that only the sons of Zadok were allowed to minister unto the Lord. The rest of the priestly family and the Levites could only minister to the house; they were not allowed to minister to the Lord.

Usually, the work of the Levites was the work of ministering unto the house. They helped the people when they came with their sacrifices. They helped them bring it to the altar, kill the sacrifice, bring the water, and so forth. The work of the Levites was to minister to the house or to the people, but the work of the priests was to minister to God, to the Lord. The priests were to burn the burnt offering, to light the candlestick of gold, to put bread on the table of shewbread, to burn incense on the golden altar of incense. They ministered unto God, and after that, they came forth and blessed the people and taught the people (see Numbers 18:1-7, II Chronicles 15:3).

But only the sons of Zadok were faithful during the general declension in Israel. At that time, even the Levites and some priests fell away to serve the idols. Those were therefore disqualified to minister unto the Lord. The sons of Zadok kept the charge during this time and were allowed to minister unto the Lord. What a privilege! But the others could only minister to the house.

What is ministering unto the Lord? It means they can draw near to the Lord; they can stand before the

Lord; they can wait upon the Lord; they can receive the Lord's Word; they can offer up to Him the fat and the blood; they can minister to Him at His table. How we need in our work to minister unto the Lord! It is not just working. We need to minister to the Lord. That has to be a most essential element in work.

Waiting Upon the Lord

How do we minister to the Lord? We wait upon Him. Oftentimes, we find the hardest thing is to wait. We are always in a hurry. We must do this; we must do that. The need is there, so we have to do it; no one else will do it. The whole world is depending on us. We cannot wait upon the Lord. We think that waiting upon the Lord is a waste of time, but to minister unto the Lord, we have to wait upon Him. We have to wait until He makes His mind known to us. We have to stand before Him.

What does this mean? In the old days, the servants, the slaves, stood there quietly with their eyes upon their master, not standing idle or passive, but they would not move until they were told either by the hand or by the eye of the master. We have to learn to stand, and we have to learn to present the fat and the blood. What is presenting the fat and the blood? In an offering, these are the two things that are offered to God—the fat and the blood. The blood is to satisfy the righteousness of God; the fat is to satisfy the love of God. We are a holy priesthood to offer spiritual sacrifices acceptable to God through Jesus Christ. We are offering the fat and the blood of the Lamb; we are offering Christ. This is our spiritual sacrifice; this is our worship.

When we are worshiping God, do you think we are sacrificing or giving ourselves to Him? The answer is both yes and no. No, in the sense that when we are offering ourselves to Him, it is actually offering Christ in us to Him. We are offering what Christ is to us to Him. We are not just offering ourselves. If we offer ourselves, we will be rejected. We are not worthy. But it is the fat and the blood of the Lamb—that which we have received. He is our nourishment; He is our cleansing; He is our food; He is our life, and because we know Him as such, we can offer it back to God. This is our spiritual sacrifice. This is our worship. *Worship is returning to God what Christ is to us*. That is worship.

How much can we worship God? It depends on how much of Christ we have received. Oftentimes, we have many words but very little worship because there is little substance. We do not know Him as we should; therefore, when we try to worship Him, it comes out in words, but the substance is not there. But still, we have to minister to the Lord, minister at His table. It means that as we commune with Him, as we believe in Him, as we receive Him, in turn we can serve Him. We cannot serve Him more than what we have believed and received from Him. Do we minister unto the Lord before we minister unto the house? What is the house today? It is the people of God. We certainly need to minister to the people of God, but before we do, we first need to minister unto the Lord himself. As we do this, it will result in ministering to the house. But it is not just ministering to the house without ministering unto the Lord.

Worship After Work

Finally, there is a parable that our Lord spoke which is rather unusual and it is recorded in Luke 17. The servant came from the field, where he had been either plowing or shepherding, after the day's work was done. He came into the house and the Lord said, "Will the master say to the servant, 'Sit down quickly and eat'? No. The master will say, 'Now go and prepare my food and serve me and after you have finished serving me, then you may go and help yourself.'"

Isn't that a strange parable? Then the Lord said, "After you have done all these things, you have to come to Me and say, 'Lord, I am but an unprofitable servant.'" What does this mean? It means that even after work, that is not the end of it. The work is done but that does not mean it is the end. After the work is done, you have to come to the Lord and minister to Him. That is worship. Worship before work; worship in work; worship after work.

It is a great temptation, after we have done the work, to say, "Well, that is the end of it. The work is done." But the Lord says, "Wait a minute; you have not served Me yet." You have to come back and say, "I am but an unprofitable servant. I did what I was told but that is nothing. I want to serve You; I want to satisfy You; I want to worship You." That should be our attitude.

Remember that everyone is a worker. All of us are engaged in the same work—the work of God. Even though we may have different responsibilities, working in different areas and having different capacities, yet our whole life is a work. We are doing God's work. We are doing the will of God, and we must do the will of God in the power of the Holy Spirit. Whatever we do, we do it in His will and in the power of the Holy Spirit. We are all engaged in His work. But does work take away our worship or does it increase our worship? If work is something you do on your own in the power of your own strength, then the more you work, the less you are able to worship. But if the work is done in His will and by His power, the more you work, the more you are able to worship. That is the difference.

So I do hope that we really see what the work of God is and how we are to do it. In doing God's work, we are just worshiping God.

7—Worship and Warfare

Exodus 20:1-6—And God spoke all these words, saying, I am Jehovah thy God, who have brought thee out of the land of Egypt, out of the house of bondage. Thou shalt have no other gods before me.

Thou shalt not make thyself any graven image, or any form of what is in the heavens above, or what is in the earth beneath, or what is in the waters under the earth: thou shalt not bow down thyself to them, nor serve them; for I, Jehovah thy God, am a jealous God, visiting the iniquity of the fathers upon the sons to the third and to the fourth generation of them that hate me, and shewing mercy unto thousands of them that love me and keep my commandments.

Deuteronomy 6:4-5—Hear, Israel: Jehovah our God is one Jehovah; and thou shalt love Jehovah thy God with all thy heart, and with all thy soul, and with all thy strength.

Matthew 4:8-10—Again the devil takes him to a very high mountain, and shews him all the kingdoms of the world, and their glory, and says to him, All these things will I give thee if, falling down thou wilt do me homage. Then says Jesus to him, Get thee away, Satan, for it is written, Thou shalt do homage to the Lord thy God, and him alone shalt thou serve.

Revelation 22:8-9—And I, John, was he who heard and saw these things. And when I heard and saw, I fell down to do homage before the feet of the angel who shewed me these things. And he says to me, See thou do it not. I am thy fellow-bondman, and the fellow-bondman of thy brethren the prophets, and of those who keep the words of this book. Do homage [worship] to God.

The word *worship* in Hebrew means "bow self down." You bow yourself down. In Greek it means "to kiss, to kiss the Son." And the word in English for worship is from the old form, "worthship." That is, He is so worthy that we must worship Him.

Who Will Be Worshiped?

We know that worship is the issue of the conflict of the ages. God and His adversary, Satan, fight over this issue of worship: Who is to be worshiped? We human beings are the battlefield, and not only the battlefield, but we are the deciding factor in that battle. Will man worship God, or will man worship the adversary? We were created as worshiping creatures. The instinct of worship is within us. We know that we are inadequate, that we must worship someone who is outside of us, who is greater, higher, and mightier than we are. And being created by God, it is but right and natural for us to worship God. If we worship God, we will find our fulfillment. But unfortunately, there is an enemy, and this enemy is trying to steal that worship which is God's due. He is trying to lead us away from worshiping God into worshiping him. That is the reason worship is the center of a tremendous conflict that is going on in this world today.

After God created Adam, He put him in the garden of Eden. He gave everything to man to enjoy but on one condition: Man must obey God. God said, "Of every tree of the garden thou shalt freely eat; (and that included the tree of life) but of the tree of the knowledge of good and evil, thou shalt not eat of it;

for in the day that thou eatest of it thou shalt certainly die" (Genesis 2:16b-17).

Why did God put this limitation upon man? Of course, there are many reasons, but one is that God put man under a condition of obedience to show him that God is God, that God is to be worshiped. In obeying the commandment of God, man worshiped God because we know that obedience is a form of worship. How do we worship God if not by obeying Him, by obeying His commandment? So God put man under that one condition of obedience because man was created as a worshiper. But we know that Satan came in and tried to share God's glory and God's worship.

You remember in Isaiah 14:13-14 those words that concern Lucifer, the archangel, and how he fell from heaven and was cast out from the presence of God because he said, "I will ascend into the heavens, I will exalt my throne above the stars of God, and I will sit upon the mount of assembly, in the recesses of the north; I will ascend above the heights of the clouds, I will be like the Most High." In other words, this archangel aspired to be equal with God. He wanted to share God's glory. He wanted to receive the worship that was God's due, and because of that, he became Satan, the adversary of God, and he was cast out from heaven.

Satan came into the garden to tempt man. Outwardly, he was suggesting to man that if they would eat the forbidden fruit, they would be like God. In other words, they would receive the glory; they could worship themselves. They did not need to worship God. But actually, if man began to worship himself, he would be worshiping the devil. How subtle was that temptation because outwardly Satan was trying to say, "You don't need to worship God; you can be sufficient in yourself. You don't need to obey anyone. You are the master. You can worship yourself. You will get all the glory." What a temptation this was! But falling into that temptation was to fall into the trap because you think you are worshiping yourself, but actually, you are worshiping Satan, the devil. Unfortunately, man fell. And because of that, throughout the ages, this matter of who man will worship has become an issue. From the day of Adam until our day, worship is the issue of the universe. Will man worship God, or will he worship Satan by worshiping himself? If man is to worship God, and that is what man should do, Satan will try every way to take that worship away. He will attack. He will use every trick that he has trying to deceive man into giving him the worship instead of giving God worship.

Worshipers Attacked By Satan

Job

In the Old Testament, you will find case after case where man, when he was on God's side and worshiping Him, was attacked by the enemy. But thank God, God's grace is sufficient. One instance of this is Job (see Job 1). He was a man who was upright and feared God. One day, Satan appeared before God, and God said, "Where have you been?"

And Satan said, "I have been going to and fro throughout the whole earth." Now he was not just traveling as a tourist, but he was observing very carefully like a lion trying to devour.

And God said, "Hast thou considered my servant Job, that there is none like him on the earth, a perfect and an upright man, one that feareth God and abstaineth from evil?" (v.8). In other words, Job was a worshiping person, one who worshiped God and, of course, Satan noticed that.

So Satan said, "Isn't there a reason why Job worships You? It is because You put a hedge around him; You protect him; You bless him; You give him much. If You take these things away, see if he will not curse You to the face."

God said, "All right, I will take the hedge off. You may do anything you want except do not touch his life." In one day, Satan attacked him again and again and took everything away from him—not only his properties but even all of his children. He was just left with himself and his wife. But the Bible says that Job said, "Naked came I out of my mother's womb, and naked shall I return thither: Jehovah gave, and Jehovah hath taken away; blessed be the name of Jehovah!" (v.21).

Another day Satan appeared before the Lord, and the Lord said, "Now what do you think? What will you say?"

Satan said, "Skin for skin, yea, all that a man hath will he give for his life; but put forth thy hand now, and touch his bone and his flesh, and see if he will not curse thee to thy face!" (Job 2:4b-5).

Then God said, "All right, you can do it, but you cannot take away his life." So Job was attacked with a grievous boil from his head to his feet, and he sat in the ashes and scraped himself with a potsherd. Even his wife said, "Curse God and die." But Job said, "We receive good from God; shall we not also receive evil?" (see Job 2:9-11). Here was a man who worshiped God in prosperity and worshiped God in adversity because God is worthy to worship.

Shadrach, Meshach, Abednego

Remember the story of Daniel's three friends, Shadrach, Meshach, and Abednego. God revealed to Nebuchadnezzar that he was the golden head, but somehow he took it wrongly. Nebuchadnezzar made a golden image of himself and sent out a proclamation that all the people, when they heard the music that was made, must bow down and worship the image. In other words, by worshiping the image, they would be worshiping Nebuchadnezzar. He did not know that it was Satan who really received the worship. But the three friends of Daniel—Shadrach, Meshach, and Abednego—would not do it because they worshiped the one and only God. So it was reported to the king, and he called the three men to him and said, "Didn't you hear the music? I will give you another chance. When the music is played, you must worship the image. If not, then you will be thrown into the fiery furnace."

Daniel's three friends replied, "Concerning the matter, there is nothing to discuss or negotiate. It is already settled. We cannot worship your image because we worship only God. And we believe that God is still able to save us, to deliver us from the furnace and deliver us from your hand." The king was so angry that he demanded the furnace to be heated seven times hotter than usual, and he threw them bound into the furnace, but the fire only burned up the ropes that bound them. And the Son of Man appeared in that furnace walking with these three men (see Daniel 2-3).

Daniel

Then look at Daniel, who was one of the prime ministers during the time of King Darius. The people were envious of Daniel and wanted to find fault with him, but they could not. Finally, they said there was only one way to find fault with him, and that was in his worship of God. The people persuaded King Darius by working on his ego. For thirty days, no one could ask anything of anyone but King Darius. You could not pray to God or gods or ask any favor of anyone because King Darius was the greatest. Of course, the king was pleased with this, and he sealed the decree. When Daniel heard about it, he went to his room, opened his window towards Jerusalem and prayed three times a day, and his enemies were watching. As a result, he was thrown into the lions' den. But God shut the lions' mouths.

Throughout the ages, worship is the issue. Who is to be worshiped? Is God to be worshiped or Satan? If anyone worships God, Satan will try in every way to get that worship away from God unto himself. This is the battle of the ages.

The Lord Jesus

But thank God, one day, one Man came into this world, and His name was Jesus. Our Lord Jesus was driven by the Holy Spirit into the desert to be tempted of the devil. The scene was so different from Adam's temptation. Adam was in the garden of Eden—a beautiful garden, one of plenty and of pleasure. It was the best of environments that God had provided for man. And Christ was in the wilderness—barren, nothing, only animals. It was the worst of environments. Adam failed when he was tempted, yet the second Man, Christ, overcame Satan when He was tempted. And those temptations came to their consummation which was actually worship. All the other things were just the fringes, but the real issue was over this matter of worship. So finally, Satan came out with boldness and showed our Lord Jesus all the kingdoms of the whole world and said, "All of these are mine." (Of course, that was a lie.) "Just bow down and worship me and you will have them all." The Lord replied, "Satan, get thee away. It is written, 'Thou shalt worship the Lord thy God and

Him alone shalt thou serve'" (see Matthew 4:9b-10). Our Lord Jesus overcame Satan. In this matter of worship, He declared that God alone is to be worshiped. This is the testimony of the new Man. We who are in Christ Jesus have this testimony with us, and our testimony is simply that God alone is to be worshiped.

The Children of Israel

Go back to the Old Testament where God delivered His people out of Egypt. He brought them to Mount Sinai, and there He gave them the Ten Commandments. As you read them, you will find the first four are really concerning this matter of worship (see Exodus 20). The first commandment says, "Thou shalt have no other gods before me" (v.3). The second commandment says, "Thou shalt not make thyself any graven image ... thou shalt not bow down thyself to them" (v.4a, 5a). God alone is to be worshiped. God redeemed a people so that they might be a worshiping people, that they might worship God as they should.

Hear, Israel: Jehovah our God is one Jehovah; and thou shalt love Jehovah thy God with all thy heart, and with all thy soul, and with all thy strength. (Deuteronomy 6:4-5)

God gave everything to His people. But there is one thing that God will never give away, and that is His glory or His worship. Brothers and sisters, our God gives us everything. There is not anything that He will not give us, but there is one thing He will never give up, that He will not share with us, and that is His worship, His glory.

This is the controversy between God and His people, Israel. If you read the history of the children of Israel, you will find that the controversy is only upon this matter of worship. The children of Israel should worship God; yet, they became unfaithful, they became idol worshipers. It was an abomination in the eyes of God. God pled with them and disciplined them, but only on this one matter of worship. Where did they fail God? They failed God in worship. Where was God's controversy with them? It was over this matter of worship. It was not over many issues or many things. It was all centered upon this matter of worship and, finally, they were taken into Babylonian captivity because they committed abominations; that is, they worshiped idols. But thank God, in the Babylonian captivity, the children of Israel were healed of their idol worship. Also, we find that by God's grace a remnant returned to Jerusalem to rebuild the temple, and the temple is the symbol of worship. Therefore, remember that worship is the issue.

A Worshiping Life

In the New Testament, you will find the same thing, but we began on better ground. With the children of Israel, God gave them commandments; He demanded worship from them. They should worship God and no one else and nothing else, and they failed. But in the New Testament, the church is not only given the command to worship God, but we are also given the life to worship God. The children of Israel were under the law, and they knew they should worship God. They were commanded to worship God; yet they failed. But we who are in the New Testament are under grace. What is grace? Grace means God not only demands but He gives us the life first. Because He gives us the life, therefore, we are able to respond to God's demand.

The life that we receive when we believe in the Lord Jesus is a worshiping life. It is the life of Christ. How our Lord Jesus worshiped God throughout His life! Not only when He was tempted in the wilderness and said, "Thou shalt worship the Lord Thy God and Him alone shalt thou serve," but throughout His life, it was a life of worship. In His actions or His reactions, in His relationships, in His daily life, in His words or in His deeds, He worshiped the Father in spirit and truth throughout His life. No matter how He was tempted, no matter how He was attacked, He worshiped God in all circumstances.

First, the enemy tried to give our Lord the whole world. He said, "If you worship me, you will get the whole world." But our Lord Jesus said, "No, the Father is more important than the world. The Father is to be worshiped" (see Matthew 4). How often Satan tries to use the world to get our worship. What is the world? The world is not just what we see; the world is not just those things that will attract the lust of the eyes, the lust of the flesh, and the pride of life (see I John 2:16). The world is not just a society or an organization. We know the world is a cosmos, a system, and Satan organized that system in order to get our worship. That is the reason the Bible says, "Love not the world because if you love the world, the love of the Father is not in you" (see I John 2:15). Whatever you love you worship. If you love the world, you worship the world; but, in worshiping the world you are worshiping Satan. If you love the Father, you worship the Father.

What worship it was when our Lord was on the cross! Satan tried to use the world to get the worship from our Lord Jesus, but he failed. So finally, he tried to stir up the world to reject and to crucify Christ, and he thought he succeeded. If you review the scene of Calvary you will find that our Lord Jesus was rejected by the world. The world was offered to Him, but He rejected it. Now the world rejected Him and He was crucified on the cross. But while He was there on the cross, He said, "Father, forgive them, for they know not what they do" (Luke 23:34). At twelve o'clock, when darkness filled heaven and earth, He cried out, "My God, my God, why hast thou forsaken me?" (Mark 15:34). Then around three o'clock, He shouted, "It is finished" (John 19:30). And with a loud voice He said, "Father, into thy hands I commit my spirit" (Luke 23:46). What is that? That is worship. Even on the cross, our Lord Jesus was worshiping the Father. There is no place where worship is manifested so fully as on Calvary's cross. Here was a Man who worshiped God even on the cross.

The life that we receive from God is this life. We have a worshiping life in us—one that worships God. We have a life in us that rejects the world, a life in us that worships God even on the cross. This is the life that we begin with; therefore, it is different from the people in the Old Testament times. We begin on higher ground. In this spiritual warfare we are on higher ground. In other words, we fight from victory to victory. Christ has already overcome Satan in this issue of worship; therefore, we start from the ground of victory in the matter of worship. We worship God and God alone. This is our testimony. What is the testimony of the church? God alone is to be worshiped. The world says worship Satan, but the church says worship God. This is where you see the conflict.

A Corporate Vessel of Worship

The conflict is going on not only on earth but in the unseen world. Review the history of the church. In the book of Acts, which is a history of the early church, what do you see? You see the church did begin as a worshiping church. They persevered in the teaching and the fellowship of the apostles, in the breaking of bread and in prayers. How they loved one another! How they exalted the name of our Lord! How they rejoiced in the grace of God! (see Acts 2).

In other words, here on earth, there is a corporate vessel and it is a vessel of worship. They worshiped God, they exalted Christ, they obeyed the Lord. Would Satan just stand by and do nothing? No! Even from the very beginning, the Jewish Council, that highest judicial authority, that religious authority, that Judaism which is supposed to worship God, began to attack first. They took Peter and John and forbade the apostles to preach in the name of the Lord Jesus. The conflict was there. You will remember that the apostles said, "If it be righteous before God to listen to you rather than to God, judge ye; for as for us we cannot refrain from speaking of the things which we have seen and heard" (Acts 4:19-20). This was an attack from the outside, from the religious world.

Very soon, you will see that Satan tried to cause problems from within—Ananias and Sapphira, or the distribution of food to the widows. Satan tried every means, both inside and outside, to destroy that testimony in order to get worship away from God to himself. But the church goes on. The church is the church triumphant! Throughout the ages it has been, and still is, the testimony of the church that God alone is to be worshiped.

The church does not have an easy time. Even towards the end of the first century you will find in the writings of Peter, Paul, and John that there was a general falling away from first love. God was not worshiped as He should have been. People began to fall into the world. Even Demas loved the world and went to Thessalonica (see II Timothy 4:10). This was the beginning of a falling away, but thank God, there is always the call of overcomers. And who are these overcomers? They are those who overcome the world and worship God as they should. Throughout the centuries, in the history of the church, we see this is the issue. Many suffer over this matter of worship. Whoever will give God all the worship, he can expect attacks not only from the world but even from the religious world.

When you come to the book of Revelation, as you read it, you see it is a book of worship. Why? Because worship is the issue. When you come to the end, that issue will be forever settled, but before that issue is to be forever settled outwardly, it has to be first settled spiritually and inwardly. That is to say, God has to get a worshiping people on earth today, and their worship will bring down the kingdom of the enemy. Their worship will prepare the way for the kingdom of God to come upon this earth so that the issue of worship will be forever settled. That is the reason our Lord Jesus said that the Father is seeking for worshipers, true worshipers, those who worship Him in spirit and truth (see John 4:23).

John said in Revelation 1, "To him who loves us, and has washed us from our sins in his blood, and made us a kingdom, priests to his God and Father: to him be the glory and the might to the ages of ages.

Amen" (Revelation 1:5b-6). John wrote this book in the spirit of worship because he saw. He saw that God was going to get all the worship.

In chapter 4, you will see the four living creatures saying, "Holy, holy, holy, Lord God Almighty" (see v.8) and the twenty-four elders bowing before the throne. Why is this? "For thou hast created all things, and for thy will they were, and they have been created" (v.11b). We see the glory of the Creator and when you see that, you cannot help but worship Him.

In chapter 5, you see the Lamb standing in the midst of the throne as newly slain. Again, you will find a new song being sung, "Thou art worthy to take the book, and to open its seals; because thou hast been slain, and hast redeemed to God, by thy blood, out of every tribe, and tongue, and people, and nation, and made them to our God kings and priests" (vv.9-10). This worship was not only done by those who are redeemed but by all the angelic hosts and even the created beings. They were worshiping God who sits on the throne and the Lamb who is in the midst of the throne. This is worship!

In chapter 7, there are numberless people, countless people, standing before the throne and before the Lamb. They have palms in their hands, and they give God and the Lamb all the glory. They are worshiping!

In chapter 11, when the seventh trumpet is sounded, immediately there is worship in heaven because the kingdom of God is coming.

In chapter 12, you will find the man child is being raptured to the throne, and while the earth will be in tribulation, there will be singing and worship in heaven.

In chapter 14, the one hundred and forty-four thousand stand on Mount Zion and "they sing a new song before the throne … and no one could learn that song save the hundred and forty-four thousand who were bought from the earth" (v.3).

In chapter 15, those "that had gained the victory" stood "upon the glass sea, having harps of God. And they sing the song of Moses bondman of God, and the song of the Lamb ..." (vv. 2b-3a) They are singing the song of the Lamb and of Moses. There again, you will find worship.

In chapter 19, you will find Hallelujah and Hallelujah and Hallelujah because the marriage of the Lamb has come. Babylon has fallen. It is worship!

Of course, when you come to the last chapter it is so glorious that John somehow got lost. He was shown all of these glorious things by the angel and he was so elated, so taken up and excited that he began to worship the angel, and immediately, the angel said, "Do not worship me. I am but a fellow-servant. Worship God" (see v.9). This is how the book of Revelation is concluded.

So dear brothers and sisters, remember one thing: Worship is the issue of the ages. We are the chosen vessel, the church, to testify to both the seen and the unseen world that God alone is to be worshiped. How effective is our testimony? It is sad when we find the church has fallen into the world. It is not just a matter of the church being worldly; it is not just a simple matter of the church becoming like a great institution in the world, but at the back of it, there is the matter of worship. When the church falls into the world and becomes worldly, God is deprived of His worship and Satan is worshiped. It is a serious matter.

Yes, it is a serious matter corporately, but it is also a serious matter personally. We have to decide before the Lord who is to be worshiped. You remember Elijah on Mount Carmel challenged the children of Israel, the chosen people of God: "How long do ye halt between two opinions? if Jehovah be God, follow him" (I Kings 18:21). It has to be settled.

Is this matter of worship a settled issue in your life? Are you still halting between two opinions—God or the world? "No one can serve two masters; for either he will hate the one and will love the other, or he will hold to the one and despise the other. Ye cannot serve God and mammon" (Matthew 6:24). Where is your heart? Remember, if you choose to worship God, it is natural because you have His life in you, and if you worship God, you will find fulfillment. In the world, it is natural for people to worship Satan because that is their life. It will be most unnatural with us if we still love the world and allow it to take away from our worshiping God.

We need to be before the Lord as individuals, as well as a corporate vessel, declaring that God alone is to be worshiped. It is true—it will be costly. You will find that you will be tempted; you will be assaulted; but thank God, our Lord Jesus has already overcome, and this overcoming life is in us. So we will overcome, and we will worship God.

Titles Available from Christian Fellowship Publishers

By Watchman Nee

Aids to "Revelation"

Amazing Grace

Back to the Cross

A Balanced Christian Life

The Better Covenant

The Body of Christ: A Reality

The Character of God's Workman

Christ the Sum of All Spiritual Things

The Church and the Work – 3 Vols

The Church in the Eternal Purpose of God

"Come, Lord Jesus"

The Communion of the Holy Spirit

**ORDER FROM: 11515 Allecingie Parkway
Richmond, VA 23235**
www.c-f-p.com – 804-794-5333

Titles Available from Christian Fellowship Publishers

The Finest of the Wheat – Vol. 1

The Finest of the Wheat – Vol. 2

From Faith to Faith

From Glory to Glory

Full of Grace and Truth – Vol. 1

Full of Grace and Truth – Vol. 2

Gleanings in the Fields of Boaz

The Glory of His Life

God's Plan and the Overcomers

God's Work

Gospel Dialogue

Grace Abounding

Grace for Grace

ORDER FROM: 11515 Allecingie Parkway
Richmond, VA 23235
www.c-f-p.com – 804-794-5333

Titles Available from Christian Fellowship Publishers

Heart to Heart Talks

Interpreting Matthew

Journeying towards the Spiritual

The King and the Kingdom of Heaven

The Latent Power of the Soul

Let Us Pray

The Life That Wins

The Lord My Portion

The Messenger of the Cross

The Ministry of God's Word

My Spiritual Journey

The Mystery of Creation

Powerful According to God

ORDER FROM: 11515 Allecingie Parkway
Richmond, VA 23235
www.c-f-p.com – 804-794-5333

Titles Available from Christian Fellowship Publishers

Practical Issues of This Life

The Prayer Ministry of the Church

The Release of the Spirit

Revive Thy Work

The Salvation of the Soul

The Secret of Christian Living

Serve in Spirit

The Spirit of Judgment

The Spirit of the Gospel

The Spirit of Wisdom and Revelation

Spiritual Authority

Spiritual Discernment

Spiritual Exercise

ORDER FROM: 11515 Allecingie Parkway
Richmond, VA 23235
www.c-f-p.com – 804-794-5333

Titles Available from Christian Fellowship Publishers

Spiritual Knowledge

The Spiritual Man

Spiritual Reality or Obsession

Take Heed

The Testimony of God

The Universal Priesthood of Believers

Whom Shall I Send?

The Word of the Cross

Worship God

Ye Search the Scriptures

ORDER FROM: 11515 Allecingie Parkway
Richmond, VA 23235
www.c-f-p.com – 804-794-5333

Titles Available from Christian Fellowship Publishers

The Basic Lesson Series by Watchman Nee

Vol. 1 - A Living Sacrifice

Vol. 2 - The Good Confession

Vol. 3 - Assembling Together

Vol. 4 - Not I, But Christ

Vol. 5 - Do All to the Glory of God

Vol. 6 - Love One Another

ORDER FROM: 11515 Allecingie Parkway
Richmond, VA 23235
www.c-f-p.com – 804-794-5333

Titles Available from Christian Fellowship Publishers

By Stephen Kaung

Abiding in God

Acts—The Working of the Holy Spirit

"But We See Jesus"—The Life of the Lord Jesus

Discipled to Christ—As Seen in the Life of Simon Peter

Elijah and Elisha—One Prophetic Ministry

God's Purpose for the Family

Government and Ministry in the Local Church

The Gymnasium of Christ

In the Footsteps of Christ

I Corinthians—Called into Fellowship

II Corinthians—A Man in Christ

Isaiah—The Redemption of the Lord

ORDER FROM: 11515 Allecingie Parkway
Richmond, VA 23235
www.c-f-p.com – 804-794-5333

Titles Available from Christian Fellowship Publishers

Shepherding

Teach Us to Pray

The Songs of Degrees—Meditations on Fifteen Psalms

The Sons of Korah

The Splendor of His Ways—Seeing the Lord's End in Job

Titus

Worship

The "God Has Spoken" Series by Stephen Kaung

Seeing Christ in the Old Testament, Part One

Seeing Christ in the Old Testament, Part Two

Seeing Christ in the New Testament

ORDER FROM: 11515 Allecingie Parkway
Richmond, VA 23235
www.c-f-p.com – 804-794-5333